beyond the picture

> We have a complex history with fishes and how we use them, and this is well reflected in the invasion pathways that alien fishes have utilised over time. Not all fishes have the potential to become invaders, but the diversity of fishes that are used and transported globally has ensured that many of the most adaptable species find their way into precisely the wrong places.

Tim Smith / Ichthyologist Page 22

Contents

Welcome

WHAT IS *fish*? This wasn't the easiest pitch to make to my publishers. It's about fish, I told them, that single word explaining both everything and nothing.

They could just as easily have asked me to define a fish. The eminent evolutionary biologist Stephen Jay Gould spent much of his working life trying to do exactly that, only to conclude that there's no such thing. He was on to something too. From a biological perspective, the catch-all term is just too broad. A salmon is a fish. A hagfish is a fish. A camel is not a fish. A salmon is more closely related to a camel than it is to a hagfish. Fish are more of a concept than a definition.

So too, *fish* is more of a concept than a definition. This is a magazine about fish in the wider concept. It is the story of the noun; the creatures we know collectively as fish. It is the story of the verb; the act of fishing. It is the story of fish in seas and in rivers, in tin cans and in art, in ecology and in law.

I keep fish. I eat fish. I have taught about fish, and perhaps still do. And what I have learned is that the subject is immense. Fish are immense. There are so many of them, some 34,000 recognised species, across so many habitats, with so many niche behaviours, that it is impossible to know them all.

The story of fish is an epic far greater than I could ever archive. But with this magazine, I hope to bring some insight into the obscure, the uncelebrated, the glorious, the tragic, the beautiful. The lives of the fishes permeate through our human culture. They reside in our myths and legends. Many towns and cities owe their existence to them. We take for granted the sustenance they bring us, from faraway peasant fisherfolk who may earn their entire income catching ornamental species for aquaria, to local seaside communities that can be bankrupted in the space of one poor harvest. Fish have brought us so much. The least we can do is learn a little of them in return.

This is not a magazine specific to marine biologists, aquarium keepers, anglers, or chefs. It is a magazine for anyone who wants to learn more of their own lives. Fish are as wondrous as they are mysterious, but their story is also our story. This is our story.

At least, it's my conception of our story.

Cover Art:
Teuthis

Nathan Hill | Editor

Charging the enemy

Electric eels turn out to be far more complex that anyone could have ever imagined.

Nathan Hill | Aquarist

ELECTRIC EELS. Long, mysterious and deadly. They can kill a man, right? *They can kill a man, right?*

Much is made of the legend, and some of it is wrong. For a start, they aren't even eels, at least not in any true sense. The resemblance is superficial; electric eels are Gymnotiformes, the Knife fish of South America. Curious-looking long fish that rely on a modified fin on the underside of the body to move about. And their ability to generate electricity isn't all that exclusive, either. Some 350 fish species can do it, though they mostly use their charge for navigation and communication.

Most of the interesting stuff about Electric eels has emerged only recently. For around 500 years we've been aware of 'the' Electric eel. In 2019 we discovered that there wasn't just the one species but at least three: *Electrophorus electricus*, *Electrophorus varii* and *Electrophorus voltai*. The discovery of *E. voltai* brought with it a new record for electric prowess — this species can discharge a phenomenal 860 Volts, compared to the 480 Volts of *E. electricus* and 572 Volts for *E. varii*.

Electric eels are practically blind, able to distinguish night from day but little else. Instead, they rely on tiny electrical pulses to create an electrical field that 'paints' the surrounding area. Anything that happens to be in their electrical field creates a shadow, and one that they can feel. To navigate, they pulse through the water, several tiny charges a second to feel the environment as they go. Zap zap zap. A little more of a charge can become enough to startle anything in the vicinity, something akin to a small static shock. When on the prowl, electric eels are known to do this to help flush out hidden prey. Zap ZAP zap. At full power and targeted, an electric eel can famously kill its prey outright. ZAP ZAP ZAP.

Electric eels may stun repeatedly before eating their prey. They rely on a delicately lined mouth to breathe — some 80% of their oxygen intake comes from gulping atmospheric air while their gills serve mainly to release carbon dioxide — and so damage to the sensitive skin here could be a problem. Prey is always handled the same way, shocked insensible and then swallowed whole, head first.

Perhaps most exciting discovery is that Electric eels hunt in packs. Collaborative hunting is rare in the animal kingdom, requiring a degree of advanced cognition and communication that most animals lack. It's so scarce amongst fish that you could count

Electric Organs (EOs)

Hunter's EO   Main EO   Sach's EO

Image: Pally /Alamy

the species that do it on both hands and still have a pinky to spare. But that's exactly what *E. voltai* have been recorded doing, over a hundred of them working together to round up small prey fish into a confined space before taking turns to shock them, the startled prey first leaping from the water before dropping back down unconscious to the waiting swarm below.

As for the charge itself, that's generated by three specialised electrical organs: Main, Hunter's and Sach's. 'Electrocyte' muscle cells make up these organs, each a tiny biological battery arranged the way AAs might be stacked in a torch. A large electric eel might have 20,000 of these cells. The Main and Hunter's organs deal with delivering shocks while Sach's organ takes care of navigation. Generating bioelectricity involves transporting potassium and sodium ions from inside to outside the electrocyte cells, after which one side of the cell (the side with a nerve attached) depolarises before the other. When all 20,000 cells do this in an orchestrated effort, the result is a powerful positive charge that races to the front of the fish, while the negative charge sinks to the tail. Anything that's between the snout and tail at that moment is about to have its day ruined.

So, *they can kill a man, right?* Actually, they can, but it's rare. A succession of shocks can result in heart failure, but it's likelier that you'd just fall unconscious and drown. An Electric eel will attack you if it feels threatened, leaping up and pressing its positively charged chin against wherever it can to deliver a tight, focused and potentially lethal shock. ∎

Above: *Most Electric eels are active at night, To find one out during daytime is unusual.*

Left: *The three electric organs combined take up some 80% of the fish's mass.*

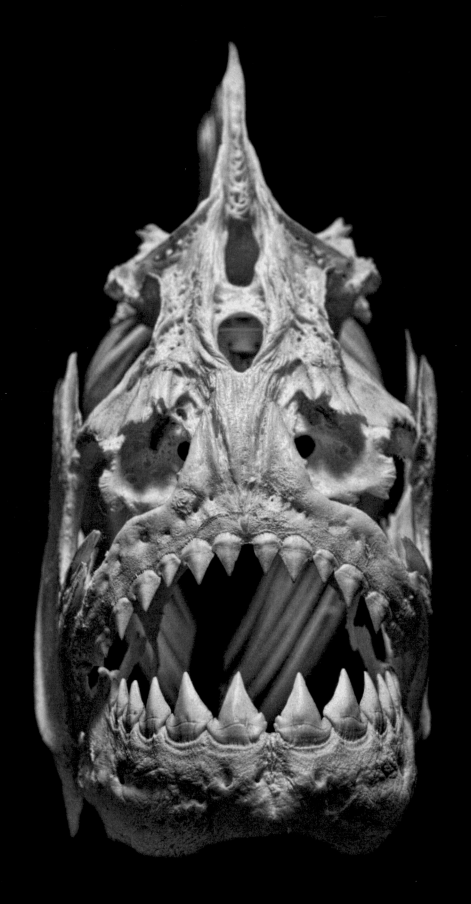

The bone hunter

How to collect piranha from Venezuelan rivers.

Ivan Mikolji | Fish From Venezuela Foundation & Frank Magallanes | Piranha specialist

Ivan Mikolji

I'M FISHING for piranhas at the edge of the Portuguesa River in the state of Cojedes, far from cities, far from civilization. The sun has been beating down on me all day, unrelenting on the exposed parts of my body, searing the skin of my neck, my arms. Sleep will be impossible later, the caress of sunburn a cruel trophy of the day's efforts.

The Portuguesa River is a highway of suspended silt, a colour between mochaccino and chocolate milkshake. The baked riverbank is made up of hot, brown dirt, powder that becomes thick, sticky clay at the edge of the murky water. This is the dry period at the end of December and the rivers are at their lowest, far from the relief and shade of the tree canopies that leer down at me from the bank's high edge.

Nobody gets in the water. The kids don't compete to find who can swim the fastest. Everyone, including the dogs, knows well enough stay out of the infested river.

There are many species of piranha native to the region, but the one that's most feared is the Black spot piranha, or Cariba, *Pygocentrus cariba*, a species with a reputation for opportunistic emasculation.

The locals call it Capaburro — the Donkey castrator — a reverential and fitting name.

Frank Magallanes

The Piranhas or Caribe of Venezuela — we pronounce the words pee-rahn-yah and kah-ree-bay — are commonly found in clearwater rivers. These habitats are crystalline, sometimes with a blue or greenish cast to them, and they lack the tannins and the humic acid that discolour and stain, creating blackwater rivers.

Piranhas are a silvery fish and considered tetras, related to the blue-and-red Neon tetras that feature heavily in hobbyists' aquaria. Many tetras are inquisitive fish, quick to examine and ready to explore any commotion in the water. Much of their world is experienced through the mouth; a nibble here, a nibble there, to see if what they encounter is edible. They'll be bold about it, pulling the hair off your arms or legs. A piranha, especially a piranha of the genus *Pygocentrus*, is not one you want to nibble at you.

There are over 65 piranha species, with only three of these considered 'true' piranha. *Pygocentrus cariba* is one of those that I do not trust, and potentially dangerous to humans. During these periods of low water, this species can be trapped away from the main river, concentrated into shrinking pools where hunger — and the potential of being bitten — is amplified. This is partly why attacks on people are becoming more regular, as the construction of dams and highways changes the very dynamics of land and water. Piranhas become trapped. Yet, even as they are trapped, they encounter more and more humans. →

Left: *Pygocentrus cariba skull.*
Image: Ivan Mikolji

To catch Portuguesa River piranhas, nobody uses fishing rods. Some opt for plastic hand reels, like a wheel from a toy scooter with the tire and spokes removed. Other hardware is even simpler; a mere stick to swivel the fishing line, like a wooden kite spool. At the end of the fishing line, it's wise to trail with a short length of galvanized fence wire — six inches is ample — which has a hook clamped at the other end. Good hooks are scarce out here in the back of beyond, and the wire serves a purpose, preventing the piranhas from biting through the fishing line and swimming away with one.

Even this does not guarantee a hook's safety. There are exceptionally large piranhas here, and while they're not quite powerful enough to scissor through the thick wire, they are at least more than capable of biting through a metal hook and cleaving it in two. It's common to see a fisherman reel in just the eyelet and a little stub.

Fishing piranhas has its tricks. Even as you cast your bait in the water, you must be alert to a bite. Piranhas have such sharp teeth that you seldom feel a hard yank when they strike. Fail to pull the line at the exact moment, and the piranhas will have your bait away. Sometimes you might stand for minutes, waiting for an attack that never comes; the piranhas took their prize mere seconds after it hit the water and you did not notice it.

Above: *A Sardinita, Triportheus sp., used as bait.*

Below: *The Portuguesa River, part of the Orinoco basin, Venezuela.*

If you're lucky enough to catch and land one, there's a rule to handling it — the rule being that you don't. Never try to grab a piranha that's flopping about on the ground. More piranha bites happen on dry land than they do underwater. And never trust a 'dead' piranha, either. No matter how much they may look as though they are with God as they lie amongst the dirt, a lot of people, including myself, soon discover that it's just a ruse, a fish playing possum, only to reanimate and bite you in the most unexpected moment.

I swing my line in a circular motion over my head and cast it as far as I can, towards the middle of the river. As soon as it lands on the water's surface, something strikes and takes it. I strike back to secure the hook and reel in my catch, but what I have is no piranha. Instead, my prize is kink-finned and long, with a head like a duck's beak. This is *Ageneiosus magoi* a member of the driftwood family of catfish, one of the few cats that have shrugged off the constraints of a nocturnal lifestyle to become active during the day. Still, I'm amazed at its audacity, hunting at the surface and right in the middle of the river — the river alive with fish hungry for flesh and donkey testicles. Usually, surface dwellers are found near the edges, where cover is abundant and where predatory aquatic leviathans with their equally massive mouths are less likely to explore.

I throw a six-foot plastic cast net into the water to catch some bait — one advantage of fishing this South American terrain is that prey fish can be found almost anywhere — and extract it from the water just as quickly, lest I catch any piranhas that might tear through it. The net brings in a haul, mainly hatchetfish of the *Triportheus* genus, silvery and deep-set fish known locally as Sardinitas. There are also young fish from two species of piranhas, the Irridescent pirambeba, *Serrasalmus irritans* and the Slender or Pike piranha, *S. elongatus*, this latter a longer and thinner fish than the thickset curs I'm here to catch. The cast net wets the dry ground, the thirsty earth sizzling as it drinks from it. I toss the small piranhas back in the water and keep a handful of the Sardinitas as bait.

> ❛The dry riverbank is made up of hot, brown dirt, powder that becomes thick, sticky clay at the edge of the murky water❜

Image: Ivan Mikolji

Pygocentrus as a genus have the greatest bite force of all the piranhas, even exceeding that of the Great white shark, *Carcharodon carcharias*. The pressure at the tip of a *Pygocentrus* tooth has little rivalry in the animal kingdom.

Playing dead is a common piranha trait seen with juveniles in particular, and the majority of piranha bites are from mishandling. Speaking from first (bitten) hand experience, the nip is so sharp and so swift that it's largely painless. The pain occurs later, once you see the blood pouring out.

Juvenile piranhas exploit very shallow areas lined with abundant aquatic plants and small fish. It is here that small piranhas and other tetras congregate in schools. Piranhas also practice a form of natural mimicry or aggressive mimicry, with the juveniles often difficult to tell apart from more distantly related tetras. This deception of physical appearance enables juvenile piranhas to mingle with potential prey species without causing alarm.

Following page: *Caribe swimming through clearer Venezuelan waters.*

→

Right: *Landed piranhas being subdued on capture.*

An intermittent breeze is the only thing making the oppressive sun bearable. Off some way to my left, I can see the Portuguesa River bridge, the bridge that takes you to the town of Arismendi, another piranha infested area. To my right there is a fallen tree, its wizened limbs sagging and groaning under the weight of the many birds that adorn them. Most perch on the lower branches, conveniently positioned to drop down and snatch small tetras from the tawny water flowing beneath.

A large Yellow-headed caracara, *Milvago chimachima*, drifts down, lands on one of the branches and starts a staring contest with me. But I flatter myself, and smile as I realise he's not looking at me at all. His eye is concentrated on my catch, the bait fish and Caribe that litter the ground around me. I pick him a medium sized piranha, throw it to the riverbank near him. He accepts, announces himself with a screech before dropping down to the ground to eat. His cry acts as a beacon, more caracaras appearing on trees high along the riverbank, starting a shrieking chorus in the canopy overhead. I grab some more piranhas and toss them to a grateful audience.

In the distance I see two locals walking towards me on the edge of the river. Again, I swing the line and cast it as far as I can towards the middle of the brown waters. I hold the line tight, my index finger feeling when it hits the bottom of the river. In seconds I feel a tug and start pulling; another hit, another wrong target.

This time it is a Four-lined pimelodus, *Pimelodus blochii*, yet another catfish, though unlike the duck-faced curiosity from earlier, this one comes with defence mechanisms. A serrated dorsal fin, barbed in a way that penetrates skin easily but exits with difficulty, comes laced with venom. When handled, the fish writhes and fights with electric tenacity, and while its sting doesn't rival the likes of the native stingrays — fish that have been known to kill unwary swimmers — it's a burn that will stay fresh in your memory for some time.

Image: Ivan Mikolji

What's strange is that it comes out whole. Usually when you catch this catfish it is eaten by the piranhas before you can take it out of the water, leaving you with the grim spectacle of a still-breathing head stuck to a hook. As a documentary maker, I don't miss the opportunity to film the fish as it flails, desperate to tack me with its weaponised fins. By the time I finish the video the locals are upon me.

They ask me what I am fishing for. I tell them I need an exceptionally large Capaburro to skeletonise for scientific reasons, and they ask if I have spare hooks and line they can use to help me fish. I give them what I have, including a thin wire I picked up in a sports store, with a lock to place the hook and a swivel. They tie everything together, load up one of the Sardinitas and start fishing next to me. I offer them lead weights but they say no; a weighted line is a line that sinks, only good for catching catfish. They swing and cast, but much closer to the shore than I had done. A bounty of piranha soon lines the riverbank

The fishermen are as swift with their catches as they are brutal, the piranhas in the air as soon as they come out of the water and whacked down into the parched earth, terminal velocity, the concussion of them hitting the ground jarring me. These piranhas will never bite again, will not flop back into the river or even play dead. They are dead, period.

But the fish they are hooking are too small, plus I need the bones intact, not pulverised. I tell them to stop thumping them and return them to the water.

Their ulterior motive for helping me is revealed. "We'll return them to our bellies!" comes their candid reply. Inside of twenty minutes, they catch more than fifteen piranhas each. Then they stop, rest their interest on my cast net instead. One of them lifts it up and they tell me to follow them.

> ❝ The fishermen are as swift with their catches as they are brutal... ❞

→

Image: Ivan Mikolji

It is well known that fish can be conditioned to feed in certain spots — just provide regular food and they will learn. Fish farmers of carp and salmonids have long used this behaviour to their advantage, though it also occurs naturally. In areas where birds congregate, a rookery of offspring sometimes falls into the river. *Pygocentrus cariba* have learned where these spots are and sit in wait for a feathered meal to fall from the skies.

Piranhas are opportunistic feeders, not wasting time to get a free meal and making sure their greedy partners do not get more than they do. Which often the bigger, stronger ones do with much relish.

Beyond using fish flesh, fishermen have several other baits available to them, including red cloth or dough balls made from banana; beyond their piscivorous image, piranhas readily eat fruit. During the Bronze age, fishermen used timbo vines and curare to poison the water, harvesting the corpses that rose to the surface, but that practise is illegal today.

Once in the boat or on land a makeshift priest — a wooden mallet or club — is used to smack the piranha hard on the head, killing the fish outright. A traditional method of dispatch, usually reserved for the more harmless fish, involved biting the fish behind the head. There are records of people doing the same with piranhas — a good technique if you want to lose part of your tongue, and some have done just that.

It is normal for the locals who live by the rivers of South America to depend on fish for their protein, and piranhas are an abundant source. A popular treat in the certain regions of the Pantanal is piranha soup. Some natives even believe it has aphrodisiac qualities. The meat of a cooked piranha is tender and white, but full of bones.

We walk until we're opposite a bridge on the riverbank and get to a small inlet. It looks like a small river or creek, a confluence merging into the larger Portuguesa River but with no apparent flowing water.

"Here are the big ones," they say, "but you have to net them, not hook them." I tell them to go for it. They cast out my net and seconds later they're pulling it back out, filled with large, dark, purple-tinged Caribe. No sooner are the fish in the net than they've shredded it, flopping out of the ruined mesh like it's a bundle of overcooked noodles.

During their breeding season, *Pygocentrus* darken to an almost black colour. They can produce several thousand eggs which the parent fish guards among the aquatic plants. Once the eggs hatch, the fry hunt amongst the foliage for crustaceans and insect larvae, an important control of mosquitos in areas where malaria is rife. Piranhas also play an important part as an indicator species, being notably absent when water quality sours or an environment becomes hostile.

Top right: *Pygocentrus teeth are concealed behind a thick lip.*

Bottom right: *In Venezuela, a fallen tree becomes a sniping position for birds.*

The piranhas thrash around, and the three of us are powerless to interfere. Even kicking them up the slanted riverbank, away from the water, will put us at risk of terrible injury. The loud, flopping sound these piranhas make on the ground is different, it's the deep thud of heavy fish; powerful flesh, muscle and teeth. All we can do is use long sticks to keep them from bounding their way back into the river, branches used as batons to restrain the writhing maelstrom. When the mass finally stills, I choose the largest one and place it in a bag. The others are taken for the fishermen's cooking pots. I give them my fishing gear, the chewed-up cast net and then drive five hours north, back home.

And that's how I got a piranha skeleton. ∎

Image: Ivan Mikolji

fit for a King

Jason Rainbow | Neil Hardy Aquatica

SOME YEARS ago, when I still worked in aquarium retail, I had the honour of supplying fish to a family of Middle Eastern Royalty from [redacted]. This family used to religiously visit me every year when staying in London and would purchase hundreds of fishes, both saltwater and fresh; these would then be shipped back to their Royal Palace for display. From colourful marine angelfish and charismatic pufferfish, to gigantic South American catfish and dainty tetras, they would unfailingly pick out our most spectacular and ostentatious wares.

This annual trolley dash for livestock would strip the long rows of sales tanks clean. Forewarned of a visit, we would ensure these aquaria were brimming with the bright, the bold, the beautiful, and the brazenly expensive. Impulse buys were expected, and money was no object.

One species alone didn't need to be on show. Every year it was a given, a standing order that was secured in advance by the family's English liaison. It was for piranha. Specifically, the Black piranha, *Serrasalmus rhombeus*, the most intimidating member of that toothy family. I was informed that it had to be the Black piranha, and the Black piranha alone. The family wanted its oppressive bulk, its distinctive bright red eye, its thuggish underslung jaw. It's a surly fish with all the charm of a violent stabbing, and it comes with one of the most powerful bites in the world.

These Royals always wanted the largest, meanest looking piranha that they could buy. Money was no object, and every year was the same, taking 15-20 of them at a time. An individual just a few inches long can easily set you back £150-£200, and ours were way bigger than the usual offerings.

I had to instruct our Brazilian fish catchers to send the biggest adult specimens they could source, which was an unusual request. Normally as an importer of aquarium fish, you ask for smaller specimens so that they are easier to resell, and most importantly, so that you get plenty of them into every box. It doesn't matter if you get a single fish in a box or several hundred, the cost of freight and shipping to bring it to the UK is the same, and that's not cheap. Simple economics dictates that it's best to get as many fish at a time as possible and divide the freight costs between them. On this occasion, I had to request that each piranha was so large that only one or two would fit in each box. It was costing me more to transport the boxes than it was for the fish inside them, a cost that the Royals absorbed without batting an eyelid.

After several years of doing this, and sometimes shipping two loads of Black piranha a year, I finally plucked up the courage to ask what the hunger was for these fish.

It turns out that the piranhas were the only species that were being kept in the personal quarters of the family in the Palace. They were there as a warning — the household staff were told in no uncertain terms that anyone ever caught stealing Palace property would have their hands held in the piranhas' tanks.

I never did find out if they ever caught a thief. ∎

Opposite page:
The Black piranha has a right end and a wrong end to be on. This is the wrong end.

Image: Dan Sullivan /Alamy

One in four million

Nathan Hill | Shark Botherer

ACCORDING TO statistics, I am an anomaly. Tallying up the figures from around the world, the chances of being bitten by a shark are in the region of one in four million. I've been bitten six times.

The claim is as asinine as it is large. Through my professional life I've worked with sharks, and all six of my bites occurred within a narrow timescale between 1995 and 1998, when I was aquarist at a public aquarium on the south coast of England. The cavalier attitude of youth, combined with inexperience and naivety, meant that my timing was frequently off when it came to hand feeding the likes of Tope, *Galeorhinus galeus*, and though the aquarium's loosely-enforced policy dictated that these sharks were to be pole-fed, the appeal of an audience — an audience often brimming with attractive female day-trippers — made the recklessness of the act impossible to resist for a red-blooded, single, twenty-something male.

Keeping sharks in captivity comes with a number of challenges, and one of those is that the water they're kept in can become depleted of various minerals. Of these, iodine deficiency tends to be the most common and problematic. Iodine is involved in thyroid function, and when it runs low a shark will develop a goitre. If you've ever seen sharks with curious lumps in their throats, like they're struggling to swallow a tennis ball, that's likely what you're seeing; the shark's thyroid gland swelling up due to a lack of iodine.

To counter that, we aquarists would supplement diets with potassium iodide in capsules, along with a whole galaxy of vitamins poked into the carcass

*Above: Tope,
Galeorhynus
galeus.*

*Opposite page:
The author in
action with a
feeding pole.*

of some tempting fish, and distributed evenly amongst the sharks on display. If you're a visitor in a public aquarium watching the sharks feed, you might wonder why sometimes — many times — the meal offered is suddenly snatched away from one keen shark in favour of another, less interested one. There's no malice in the act, it's just a frustrated shark-keeper trying to get the right vitamins and minerals into the right fish.

It's during a perfect storm of distraction and machismo that careless aquarists get bitten. I've spoken to a fair few other shark-keepers over the years, and it seems we're all prone to 'shark blindness' in our desperation to get the right fish fed. Even with a trained eye, it can be hard to tell through the glare of high-powered lighting, the shimmer of water, and the clouds of other excited fish gathered around the feeding platform, exactly which shark is which. Being able to tell individuals apart is a marketable skill in itself, I promise you.

When you've spotted the shark you want, you tend to track it with a single purpose, numb to everything else. If you're particularly young and dumb, trying to do that by hand, and your co-worker is already distracted by the woman you're hoping to impress in the viewing tunnel below, you don't even get a warning. A sneaky five-foot Tope creeps up behind you, the loaded fish gets yanked from your grip, and the only blessing is that you don't feel anything.

That's the key thing with a shark bite. Not once did I ever feel the cut, the teeth are that sharp. Pulled out of the water, my hand would get a couple of seconds grace before the bleeding began and loud swearing followed, bellowed into the unique echoey acoustics found above all gigantic display tanks.

The insides of many public aquaria in the 1990s were speckled with testosterone filled blood. ■

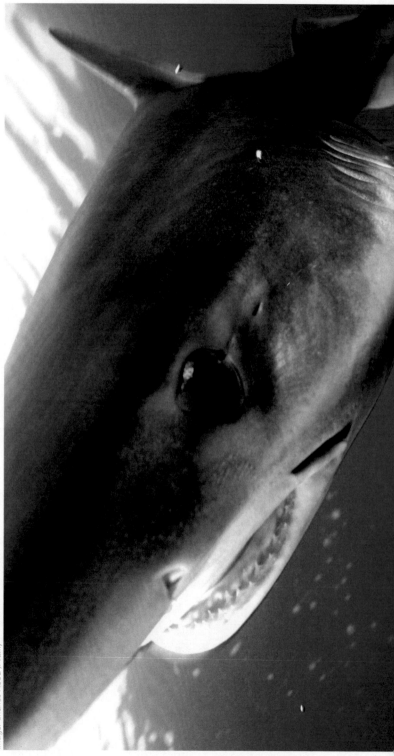

Image: Charles Hood / Alamy

Not Welcome

When predators find their way into waters beyond their natural range, they can severely impact ecosystems and blight indigenous populations. While control in some instances can be as simple as removal, in others it can be a complex and nuanced issue.

Tim Smith | Ichthyologist

Invasive
Lionfish are
collected on
a spear off of
North America. →

Image: ZUMA Press Inc. /Alamy

FOR ALL our accomplishments, humans can't seem to get some simple things right. The repeated introductions of non-native species to new environments, whether intentional or not, has had catastrophic consequences the world over. Animal invasions in the aquatic realm alone have been responsible for or contributed to the extinctions of several hundred species, along with the imperilment of countless others as they continue their spread.

While an invader may impose negative effects on their new environment in a number of ways, perhaps the most blatant and brutal evidence of invasive impact is the predation of the native fauna.

The act of eating your way through an ecosystem is a display of uncontested dominance. This is a characteristic typical of invasive species, wherein the invader lacks its own natural predators and native species themselves don't recognise the alien as a predator — at least until it is far too late.

There are many ways in which a predator may invade a novel ecosystem; unfortunately, there are very few examples of how to effectively control these species once they're established. Understanding these pathways and enacting efficient prevention methods are important steps towards ensuring these same mistakes are not repeated in the future.

We have a complex history with fishes and how we use them, and this is well reflected in the invasion pathways that alien fishes have utilised over time. Not all fishes have the potential to become invaders, but the diversity of fishes that are used and transported globally has ensured that many of the most adaptable species find their way into precisely the wrong places.

The Aquarium Trade

Recent events of the last few decades have seen attention turning increasingly towards the aquarium industry as a source of invasive species. Although they do not make up the bulk of introduced species worldwide, they can still be devastating, and those that have established have become some of the most serious invaders to date.

Large predators often sold for aquaria regularly find their way into the wild, usually because their owners can no longer house them, they become too aggressive or predatory, or quite simply the owner no longer holds interest. It is remarkably difficult to rehome such a fish. Many aquatic stores won't take them in since they're difficult to re-sell, and public aquaria are already inundated with monstrous aquatic pets. With no options left and unaware of the consequences, these animals are released in new places to call home. On occasion, aquarium inhabitants escape through other means, such as containment breakage during large natural disasters or through accidental discharge with waste water. The famous Lionfish invasion is believed to have started off with a few aquarium escapees, and the fish is now a problem across over 20 countries and islands along the eastern coast of the Americas.

Predacious aquarium fishes are becoming increasingly common invaders in tropical regions, and warmer countries with tropical climes like Brazil and the Philippines have seen several large aquarium species emerge as growing concerns for the well-being of native fishes.

Food and Fisheries

Introduced food fishes make their way into local systems either through direct stocking, or via aquaculture practices, which in turn may actively stock local systems or see the animals enter them through escape.

Above: Lionfish prepared in an American restaurant.

Image: Design Pics Inc /Alamy

Right:
*Introduced
for sport,
Rainbow trout
have brought
ecological
havoc.*

These fish, once established, often become integral to the lifestyles of the local people, and may furthermore represent a major economic contribution to the region. Most control methods run contrary to the livelihood of those dependent on the resource, and careful management is required to meet the needs of all parties.

Sport Fishing

In the heyday of colonial settlement, many fishes were introduced to new lands since the settlers were more familiar with species from their home country. These imported fishes were believed to be of superior fishing quality, and were introduced where 'fine sport fishing species' did not occur. Of course, these particular waters lacked many naturally occurring large predators whatsoever and the native species, having evolved in the absence of big piscivorous fish, were vulnerable to being eaten and dropped off drastically in number.

We still see similar motivations put up to this day. Large, exotic species are in demand in some south-east Asian countries, which now host a variety of huge, non-native fishes known to put up a good fight.

***

In many instances, complete eradication of an invasive species is either not possible or simply unfeasible. In the face of this, scientists and conservationists turn to other control methods in the hope of minimising the ecological damage as far as possible.

Many invaders are fiercely protected by locals who might view them as a resource, either as food or as sport. Removal would have social and economic repercussions, with scientists often receiving strong push-back from stakeholders. As if to rub salt in the wound, many countries still have active aquaculture and stocking practices in place to keep these industries alive, although we're increasingly seeing stricter legislature to prevent the problem from spreading further.

There are few methodologies that specifically remove the invader while having little to no effect on native fish populations. Targeted removal is often costly and time-consuming, but spares the cohabiting native species and environment from spill-over effects. Targeted fisheries are a good example of this, which can be further strengthened by facilitating the species' use as a resource, usually encouraging locals to consume their catches. This puts a predation pressure on the invaders where local species may not be able to, and can help prevent or stabilize the population booms that are common among invaders.

In the worst-case scenarios, some agencies may give in to the 'nuclear' option, annihilating most aquatic life in a given area. Usually these environments are so far gone that there are few native fish remaining to worry about. The usual method sees the workers poisoning a whole stretch of river, killing invader and indigenous species alike. The end-point of the poisoned location is detoxified to prevent damage to downstream ecosystems. Once they're sure that the invader has been removed, reintroduction of native species can begin. This is done through deliberate restocking efforts, or by allowing nature to take its course, where new individuals move in from further upstream. The next part of the job is ensuring that this 'clean slate' is not re-invaded.

Prevention is better than the cure, as they say, and huge efforts are being made to prevent the establishment of any more invaders. Stricter controls in local legislature and increased biosecurity at both borders and aquaculture facilities are but a few ways that new invaders are stopped at the door. Continued education on the dangers of invasive species, as well as teaching communities how to get involved in an invader's removal, are critical components to successfully dealing with the problem.

The Worst Offenders

Nile Perch, *Lates niloticus*

Although this species has not seen introductions across a vast range like others in this article, the resultant death toll has been horrific. The Nile perch has been responsible for the extinction of more than 200 species of cichlids endemic to Lake Victoria, with the remaining survivors continuing to be at risk of predation.

Perhaps most unsettling is not the number of species that we know we have lost, but the countless others that have vanished undetected. Lake Victoria, with a unique population of cichlids that have been evolving their way through the lake for millennia, was beloved by taxonomists for the countless species yet to be discovered. When the Nile perch population boomed towards the end of the 1980's, some of those species were doubtlessly lost before anyone had even laid their eyes on them. Some species, many still undescribed by science, now exist only as captive populations within public aquaria or the tanks of dedicated aquarium enthusiasts. Whether these species will ever see Lake Victoria again, or if the lake will ever be suitable for reintroduction efforts, remains to be seen.

The Nile perch was introduced into Lake Victoria to provide a suitable fishery for the local populace, in place of the much smaller native cichlids. Although introduced in the early 1950's, it wasn't until decades later that the Nile perch numbers surged. Extensive fisheries on the lake appear to help keep those numbers in check, but the damage that has been done cannot be reversed. The fishery currently supports the livelihoods of countless families along the lake shore, and so the invader has become crucially interlinked with the livelihoods of these communities.

> 6 The name largemouth is not wasted. You'd be hard pressed to find many prey items that can't fit into a bass' maw. 9

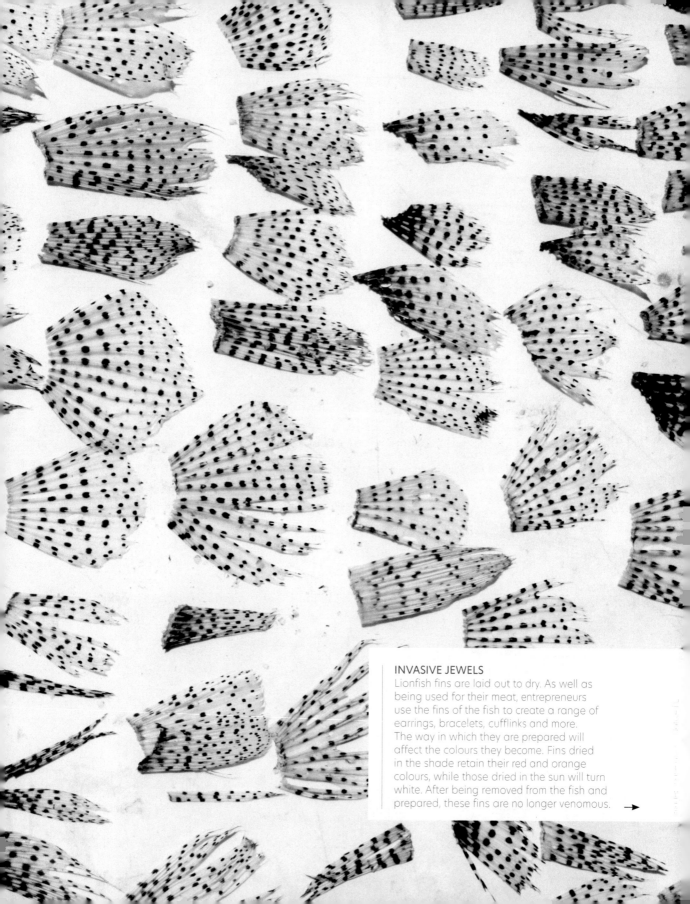

INVASIVE JEWELS
Lionfish fins are laid out to dry. As well as being used for their meat, entrepreneurs use the fins of the fish to create a range of earrings, bracelets, cufflinks and more. The way in which they are prepared will affect the colours they become. Fins dried in the shade retain their red and orange colours, while those dried in the sun will turn white. After being removed from the fish and prepared, these fins are no longer venomous. →

Rainbow Trout, *Oncorhynchus mykiss*

This is one of several salmonid species that have seen widespread introductions, although in terms of impacts it likely outshines its close relatives. Part of the Rainbow trout's success is owed to its greater tolerance for warmer waters than other trout, a trait that can be used for easier introductions as well as greater distribution throughout systems.

Spread far and wide by the demands of sport anglers, the Rainbow trout is well-established in cool, clear, unpolluted streams in nearly 100 countries. Purposeful stocking of the species continues to this day, alongside escapees from aquaculture facilities and translocations by enamoured fisherfolk.

Fast and efficient predators, trout have been linked to the decline and extirpation of a number of fish, amphibians, and aquatic invertebrates, changing ecosystem dynamics in the process and doing a poor job of replacing the species they push out. These impacts tend to affect localised, high-altitude species, which have limited ranges and may take years to recover from invader effects, if ever at all.

The trout sport fishery and aquaculture market have a few billion dollars behind them, contributing significantly to the economies of many regions. Some countries have placed controls and restrictions on where trout may continue to be stocked and managed, limiting introduction into novel systems and attempting to prevent further spread within the systems in which they are established.

Above: *Nile perch caught at the shores of Lake Victoria.*

Left: *Northern snakeheads will even survive under ice.*

Opposite page: *Young Rainbow trout are ravenous.*

Image: Paulo Oliveira / Alamy

Largemouth Bass, *Micropterus salmoides*

This American-at-large holds a special place in the hearts of countless fisherfolk, a love which has earned this species (and indeed, several other species of *Micropterus*) passage to more than 70 countries around the world, having now established in most of these.

Settling in has been made much easier with the widespread use of damming in most regions, which creates the more favourable still-water environments that most bass know and love.

The name Largemouth is not wasted. You'd be hard pressed to find many prey items that can't fit into a bass' maw. The consumption of both fish and macroinvertebrate prey has a cascading effect that alters entire community structures, often leaving the invaded environment unrecognisable within a few generations. Even larger species eventually lose the fight. Regardless of spawning successes, the resultant fry and young almost inevitably fall victim to the bass' enormous appetite. Without young to replenish the population, the ageing demographic of the native fish cannot sustain themselves in the long-term. Bass establishments can all but eliminate fishes from a stretch of river, and further fragment and isolate the surviving populations.

Bass fisheries remain popular in spite of their environmental impacts, with management and control options requiring a fine balancing act between the demands of stakeholders and environmentalists. Regardless, Largemouth bass are regularly translocated to new systems in the hopes of establishing even more fishing grounds, which usually plays out as it has in most other instances.

Lionfishes, *Pterois miles* and *Pterois volitans*

Perhaps the most rapidly-spreading invasive fishes to date, lionfishes have expanded from a likely origin in Florida to as far north as North Carolina and as far south as Brazil in just over 20 years. Their spread will likely continue until they meet an unsuitable environment, although until this point a lack of natural predators and disease has allowed their range to grow uninhibited, with feral populations that dwarf those in their native home ranges.

Having now become a transboundary problem, the odds of establishing any sort of control seems unlikely. Any areas not enforcing effective control

→

methods become refuges for later range expansion; cooperation on such a scale is not impossible, but remains incredibly difficult.

A number of efforts have been made to slow the spread and population explosions of these predators, with mixed success. Countries across their new range have attempted to market lionfishes as viable fisheries, pushed further in some regions by community-driven lionfish hunting derbies which can have dramatic effects on their numbers.

Still, these invaders have proven difficult to pin down, and while authorities are trying to determine the best management strategies, prey populations on certain reefs have declined some 80%, with other environments seeing major shifts in species composition and functioning after *Pterois* move in.

The Snakeheads, *Channa* spp.

In the early 2000's, the discovery of a breeding population of Northern snakehead, *Channa argus*, in Maryland USA caused a major stir. Certainly not a good sign, however it was unknown to most that snakeheads had been reported state-wide going back a few decades as isolated cases. Blotched snakehead, *Channa maculata*, had been established in Hawaii for over a century. Further abroad, snakeheads across Asia have been making themselves at home in river systems far from their native territories.

Below: Largemouth bass will even consume waterfowl.

Image: Paulo Oliveira / Alamy

The blame for these introductions has been pointed at both aquarium hobbyists as well as the live food market, of which both industries have seen chokehold restrictions on the importation and movement of snakeheads across borders (*Channa argus* is banned in England and Wales, while all *Channa* require licenses to keep in Scotland). Other uninvaded countries have taken similar precautions to prevent importation and subsequent invasion.

Today, at least four species of snakehead have been reported from the United States; thankfully in many instances these are not established populations. Snakeheads are capable predators of both invertebrates and fishes, with some invading species reaching sizes that leave few prey items out of reach. Snakeheads are able to breathe atmospheric oxygen, as well as travel over land should conditions be wet enough. These characteristics combined allow these unfussed predators to spread to new systems regardless of human intervention, as well as out-compete native species when water conditions become less favourable.

The impacts so far have not been severe, or at least so apparent, but there remains a worrying prospect that these repeated, isolated reports of snakehead discoveries represent regular releases by uninfomed parties. This raises concerns about new areas of establishment, as well as the efficacy of enforcement of the laws that are supposed to be keeping these invaders out. ∎

Image: Shutterstock

Above: *Naive fish have no defences against an invasive Lionfish.*

Below: *A Bullfrog is no match for a hungry Channa argus.*

The Bengal Channa

Sayantani Mahapatra | A Homemaker's Diary

THE BIG fish head on the platter for an infant's first rice eating ceremony. The live Murrel that a new bride has to hold while entering her new home, and the fish that the daughter of a deceased mother presents to the priest's feet. All of these rituals involve a Striped snakehead, *Channa striata*. And all help the Bengali Hindu community to celebrate and mourn the circle of life.

Bengalis are the third largest ethnic group in the world. Most of the Bengali Hindu people live in West Bengal, a small state on the eastern part of India, surrounded by oceans and crisscrossed by rivers.

Like any other culture that evolved around rivers and oceans, Bengalis were fond of the fish and rice that grew abundantly on the fertile riverine plains. Over time this habit grew into tradition, and the tradition became culture that governed the behaviour of this ethnic society as a whole.

Every ancient culture worships the forces and creatures of nature in some form, and one of the earliest references to that in Hinduism is in the hymns of the Rigveda, one of four canonical texts.

According to this text, Lord Vishnu took ten incarnations across different eras to save life on Earth. His first incarnation was that of the Matsya Avatar, Matsya being Sanskrit for fish. The story is very similar to that of Noah's Ark; the Matsya Avatar asked Manu — the first man — to collect all creatures of the world. When a deluge then came, Vishnu appeared as a giant, horned fish, to which Manu tied the ship with all the animals and plants.

These went on to restore life on Earth.

The majority of the world believes that Hindus practice vegetarianism but this isn't a prerequisite, and among Bengali Hindus even the Brahmin priests consume fish. Rather, the fish is an auspicious symbol for them. Every new beginning is marked by serving the largest fish head found in the market, while a wedding is never complete without the gift of a whole fish decorated with turmeric and vermillion from the groom's side. This gift represents his commitment to take good care of his bride.

Among the many games that make up a new bride's welcome ritual, the most important involves catching a live fish from a small tank, and frequently that fish is a *Channa*, slimy and difficult to hold. Blessed is a bride who can restrain it, for she will never let the happiness of her new family slip away.

But when the journey of life ends, a ten-day mourning period is observed by abstaining from eating fish. On the eleventh day a whole fish is offered to the priest and the family comes together to eat it, simply with rice.

Any ritual becomes an intrinsic part of a living and breathing culture only when it can make its adherents acutely aware of their environment. With connection to divinity and folklore, Bengali rituals do exactly that.

There are rituals that refrain people from catching fish during the breeding season, specific celebrations that mark the end to catching certain species of fish. Therein we find the beauty of faith, in its power to protect and restore ecological balance.

RECIPE

Channa striata curry with broad beans
An everyday Bengali recipe. Pairs really well with steamed rice.

INGREDIENTS:

4 *Channa striata* steaks
1 cup broad beans
1 medium onion
4-5 cloves garlic
1/2 tsp red chilli powder

1 small tomato, chopped
4-5 green chillies
3 tbsp oil
Turmeric powder
Salt

METHOD:

1. Wash the broad beans under running water and boil them in water for 4-5 minutes. Drain and allow to cool, then peel the waxy skins.

2. Grind the onion and garlic to a smooth paste.

3. Smear salt and turmeric on the fish pieces, and keep aside for 15 minutes.

4. Heat the oil in a heavy-bottomed pot and fry the fish pieces for 2 minutes on each side on medium flame. Take out.

5. In the same oil add the onion and garlic paste along with salt and chilli powder. Cook on a medium heat for 4-5 minutes until oil oozes out on the sides.

6. Add turmeric and the chopped tomato. Cook again on a low heat until the tomato is mixed through and oil starts to separate. Do not rush this step or the flavour won't be satisfying.

7. Add the peeled beans and mix. Over a low flame, cover the pan and let it cook for 5 minutes. Then add a cup of water and the fish pieces.

8. Adjust seasoning to taste and add the green chillies. I always add the chillies slightly slit at the stem side for flavour. Cover and cook on a medium heat for 6-8 minutes or until the gravy thickens and the beans are cooked.

9. Finish with a sprinkling of fresh coriander leaves. ∎

filleted Lions

Tim Smith | Ichthyologist

I N THE natural order of things, any given entity is inevitably consumed by something else. This works well the world over, and has done so since life first developed an appetite. The wheels only fall off when this cycle is interrupted.

Ah, the Lionfish, *Pterois volitans*. The now (in)famous invader of the eastern seaboard of the United States. And Central America. Oh, and as far south as Brazil. The spread of this invasive fish has been completely uninhibited thanks to a lack of savvy predators in its new territory. In its native waters across the Indo-Pacific, the Lionfish is readily taken by all sorts of large reef fish. But the dominant predators of the Atlantic — the sharks, groupers, and eels — don't quite know what to make of this hard-to-swallow newcomer. With dazzling patterning and envenoming spines, it's a dish that requires some figuring out.

Without naturally occurring predators to keep the numbers in check, Lionfish populations have exploded. This kind of demographic growth forces them to spread to other areas in search of new food sources and habitats. The predators living in these regions, too, cannot make head, tail or dinner of their new neighbour.

That's where humans come in. Where our insatiable appetites have been the downfall of countless species, they're finally in a position to do some good. Lionfish are, spikes and adornments aside, extremely palatable fish. The most efficient means of turning the tables on this invasion may be as simple as putting a fork through the invader.

Across the invaded range, local governments and NGOs have been pushing for citizens, restaurants, and fishmongers to offer Lionfish on a plate wherever possible. These efforts are to help bring nature's cycle back to a closed loop, and hopefully, bring down the Lionfish populations enough to slow their spread. It's unlikely to collapse the invading population entirely, but it's a small victory in the grand scheme of managing an unwanted alien species.

To help move thing along, here's a simple recipe for Lionfish fillets. But don't stop here — these fish fit well into many other seafood dishes, and the more you experiment in the kitchen, the more your help fight for a good cause. Tame the lion. Eat the lion.

RECIPE

Lionfish fillets with lemon butter sauce
A simple evening meal that pairs with chips and white wine.

INGREDIENTS (FILLET):
2 Lionfish fillets from the
   Western Atlantic
1 pinch salt
1 pinch fine black pepper
1 pinch paprika
1 tbsp white flour
2 tbsp oil of your choosing

INGREDIENTS (SAUCE):
4 tbsp butter
1 tbsp lemon juice
1 pinch salt
1 pinch fine black pepper
1 pinch garlic paste

METHOD:
1. Start with the sauce. Melt the butter on a medium heat until no solids remain, stirring occasionally. A slight nutty aroma indicates it is ready to be removed from the heat.

2. Mix in all other ingredients and leave on a low heat until the fish is ready to be served.

3. Moving on to the fish, dry off each fillet with a paper towel.

4. Mix your salt, pepper, and paprika together and massage into the fillets. Since we have a sauce, just some salt and pepper with a touch of paprika are suitable here.

5. Dredge the seasoned fillets in flour, being sure to cover the surfaces well.

6. Allow the oil in the pan to heat until a very light smoke is seen.

7. Add the fish to the hot oil, allowing it to sit for 2-3 minutes per side depending on the size of the fish. The flesh should appear golden when you turn it over.

8. Remove from the pan when both sides are a nice even gold. Use a paper towel to remove any excess oil.

9. Drizzle the fillets with the butter lemon sauce and serve. Lionfish fillets pair well with a serving of chips and a glass of white wine. ∎

PREP SAFETY
The dorsal and anal fins contain the infamous venom glands, and should be removed with a good pair of kitchen scissors. Remove the pectoral fins too, since they tend to get in the way.

Once removed, these venomous structures can be tossed into boiling water to deactivate the proteins in the venom. Be sure to safely discard them afterwards. Wrapping them in paper is usually good enough.

geometric Oceanographic

Teuthis | Artist

FOR ALMOST a decade across Le Havre and Paris, French pedestrians have been waking up to find the streets converted to an urban gallery of underwater art. The enigmatic Teuthis — the name could refer to anything from squid to tangs to ancient Arcadian cities — is the man behind this work of guerrilla oceanic awareness. We tracked him down to showcase his magnificent art and ask him about his methods and background.

Fish: How did you decide upon sea life as a medium to work with?

Teuthis: I grew up near the Normandy docks, spending much of my developmental life fishing and observing the local marine life. At that same time, I have always been interested in old naturalist books, as well as museums and aquariums.

I studied oceanography in Paris, and that led me to work at the Roscoff biological station on the northern coast of Brittany. Whilst there I was in direct contact with some of the most beautiful coastlines of France, but I also spent time in Australia to study the migration of rays and sharks.

In short, aquatic life left an indelible and permanent mark on my mind.

What's your present relationship with fish? Do you keep, eat, or catch them?

I do fish, and most of the time I practice catch and release, especially with freshwater species. For me, fishing mainly presents an opportunity to observe the beauty of nature; the real trophies of my fishing come in the form of the photographs I take of my catches, images that I later use as inspiration for my drawings. Regarding eating fish, I only ever keep big sea bass and soles that I catch to share with family and friends. These are the tastiest of all the fish in Le Havre's waters.

Can you describe your work process in terms of composing an image?

My process is simple. I'm inspired by the exact shapes of species I like, and then add a unique geometric touch to give them dynamism and depth. The colours I use are inspired by the urban environment of my home city — predominantly shades of brown and grey.

What artistic tools do you use?

I use alcohol markers, ink and pencil on heavy Canson paper. Usually, my original drawings are quite small, just A4 or A3, but I can then scan them to enlarge them and use them to create huge printed paste-ups for use in street art.

Lionfish/*Pterois volitans*

The invasive but beautiful Lionfish is an age-old favourite amongst fishkeepers with saltwater aquaria. When threatened, it can deliver a powerful venom through the spines in the top of its body.

> ❛ I'm inspired by the exact shapes of species I like, and then add a unique geometric touch to give them dynamism and depth. ❜

Which other artists have inspired you?

In my youth I was inspired by the graffiti painters of my neighbourhood, artists like Jace and Nefaze, but my background of studying oceanography necessarily directed me to the naturalistic and anatomically correct drawings of Charles Alexandre Lesueur and Ernst Haeckel. Today, I particularly like the work of Roa and Amok Island who mix species imagery with street art.

How long have you been developing your style?

I've been involved with graffiti since I was a teenager, but my present style — the mix of graphic with scientific and aquatic influences you can see today — harkens from 2013.

Would you consider your work to be more street or gallery culture?

Street and gallery art are two aspects of my work and that must be seen as a complete package and not separated. All of my small original drawings are intended to be seen in galleries by an attentive eye, while all of my paste-ups are made to be in the streets to impress passers-by. The two parts lead to the awareness of biodiversity, and in turn an awareness of its beauty and fragility.

What is your favourite work you've created so far?

That honour probably goes to one of my biggest projects to date — a giant squid struggling with a sperm whale on the entrance of the National Museum of Natural History of Paris. I am so proud to be a part of this beautiful place where I once studied comparative anatomy.

Where can people see your work? And how can they purchase it from you?

You can see my work in real life in the streets of Le Havre (where the largest body of it is found) as well as Paris and Reunion Island but my Instagram is probably the best tool to keep an eye on my work, especially with the ongoing health crisis.

→

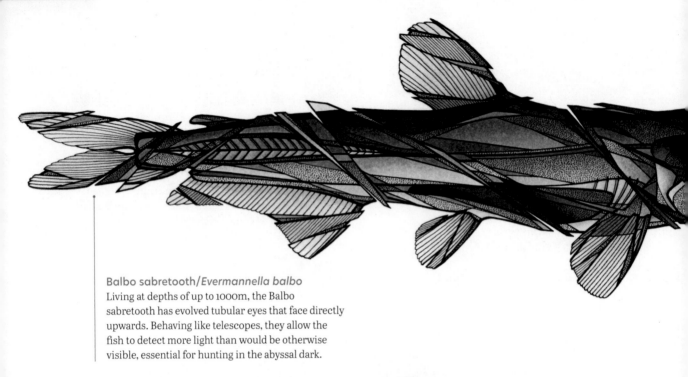

Balbo sabretooth/*Evermannella balbo*
Living at depths of up to 1000m, the Balbo sabretooth has evolved tubular eyes that face directly upwards. Behaving like telescopes, they allow the fish to detect more light than would be otherwise visible, essential for hunting in the abyssal dark.

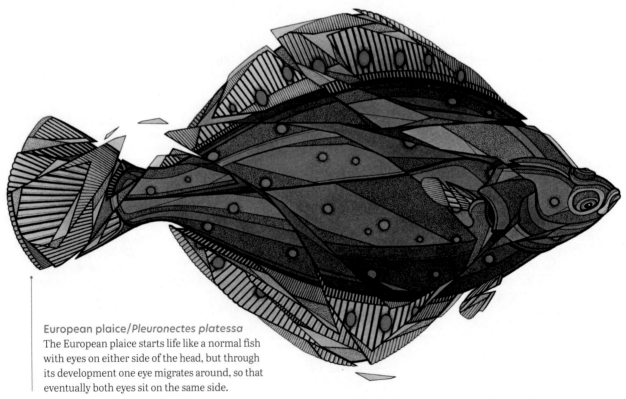

European plaice/*Pleuronectes platessa*
The European plaice starts life like a normal fish with eyes on either side of the head, but through its development one eye migrates around, so that eventually both eyes sit on the same side.

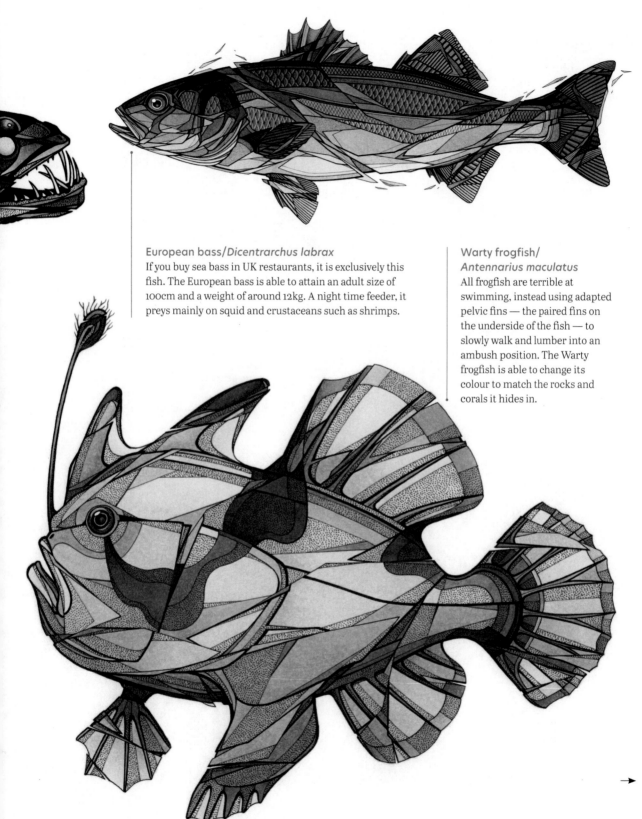

European bass/*Dicentrarchus labrax*
If you buy sea bass in UK restaurants, it is exclusively this fish. The European bass is able to attain an adult size of 100cm and a weight of around 12kg. A night time feeder, it preys mainly on squid and crustaceans such as shrimps.

**Warty frogfish/
*Antennarius maculatus***
All frogfish are terrible at swimming, instead using adapted pelvic fins — the paired fins on the underside of the fish — to slowly walk and lumber into an ambush position. The Warty frogfish is able to change its colour to match the rocks and corals it hides in.

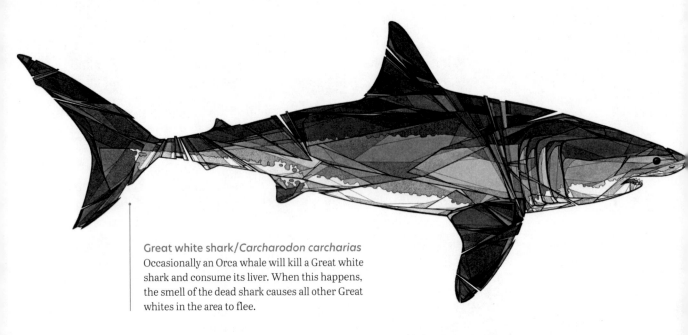

Great white shark/*Carcharodon carcharias*
Occasionally an Orca whale will kill a Great white
shark and consume its liver. When this happens,
the smell of the dead shark causes all other Great
whites in the area to flee.

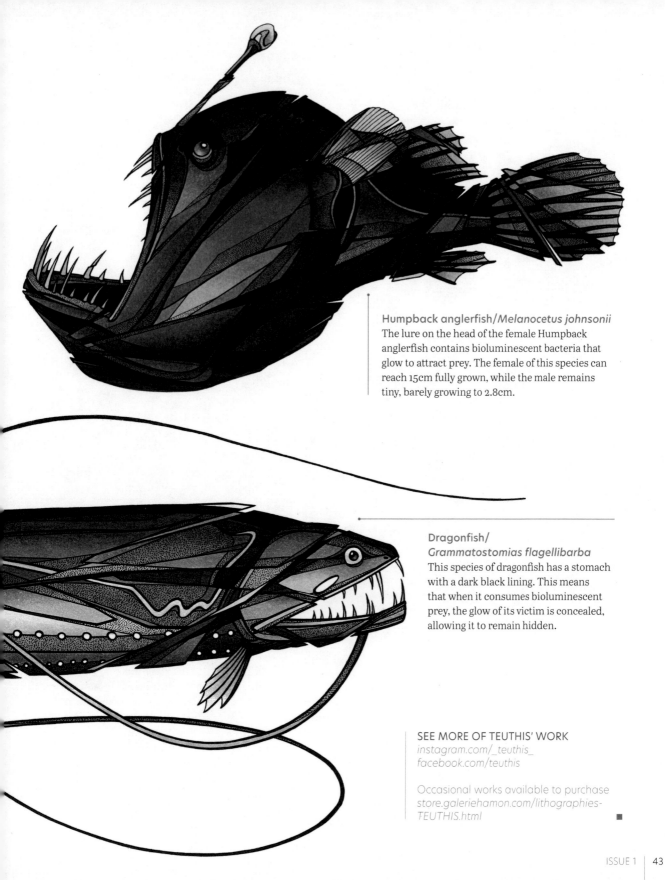

Humpback anglerfish/*Melanocetus johnsonii*
The lure on the head of the female Humpback anglerfish contains bioluminescent bacteria that glow to attract prey. The female of this species can reach 15cm fully grown, while the male remains tiny, barely growing to 2.8cm.

Dragonfish/
Grammatostomias flagellibarba
This species of dragonfish has a stomach with a dark black lining. This means that when it consumes bioluminescent prey, the glow of its victim is concealed, allowing it to remain hidden.

SEE MORE OF TEUTHIS' WORK
*instagram.com/_teuthis_*
facebook.com/teuthis

Occasional works available to purchase
store.galeriehamon.com/lithographies-TEUTHIS.html

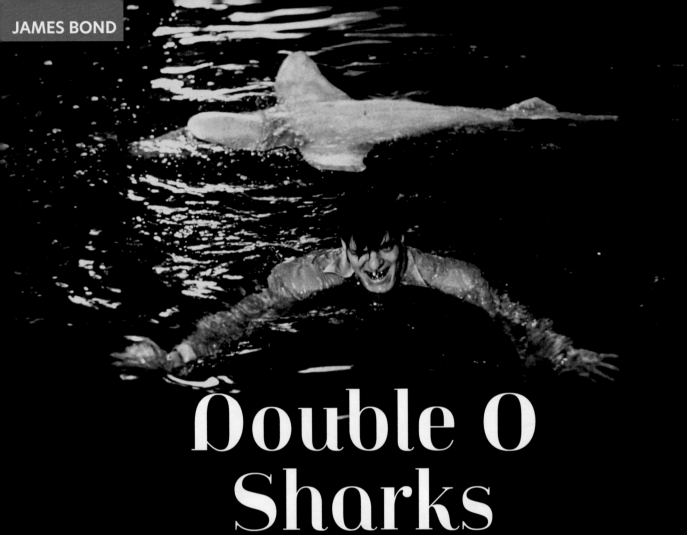

Double O Sharks

Killer shark pools have featured in no less than four
Bond films. And they've all been pretty absurd.

THUNDERBALL, 1965

"The notorious Golden Grotto sharks. The most
savage, the most dangerous. They know when it's
time for them to be fed," bragged Emilio Largo to
Bond in his Bahaman lair. A cool story but flawed
— Golden Grotto sharks don't exist. Instead, the
filmmakers opted for Tiger sharks, which was a fair
move as Tigers are definitely up there as one of the
likelier species to attack humans.

That must have been of little reassurance to
actor Sean Connery. In one scene, he has to open
a submerged hatch to swim through a shark tank,

having just seen off one of Largo's henchmen.
The idea was that this scene would all be filmed
underwater, and the sharks would be separated
from the cameraman and Connery by thick Perspex
sheets. The problem was, the guys making the props
couldn't get sheets large enough for the job, and in
the event the sharks got over the top of it. That scene
where Connery opens the underwater hatch and a
shark comes along? That was a screw up, and the
fear on Connery's face is apparently very real. Worse
still, when he swam into the tunnel, there was yet
another shark swimming down to greet him.

LIVE AND LET DIE, 1973

Definitely up there as a moment of pure absurdity, the demise of Dr Kananga involved a shark tank but less shark — the animatronic rubber model built for the scene refused to work properly, and even when it did, the shark expert on set protested at how bad it looked. The original script called for Bond to shove a compressed CO_2 'bullet' into the shark's mouth, for it to then swim away and blow up. In the event they bypassed that and went for a scene with the bullet going straight into Kananga's mouth, resulting in a few seconds of historic cinema cringe.

Cue a couple of spliced scenes from a public aquarium, so dark that it's tricky to work out exactly what species they were trying to suggest, and it was a wrap. I'll be candid, with the broad snout and head shape that can be made out, the smart money is on another Tiger shark.

The next time you watch Spielberg's 'Jaws', take note of the car number plate taken out of the autopsied Tiger shark; it's a nod to Live And Let Die, with a whole heap of subtle easter eggs attached.

THE SPY WHO LOVED ME, 1977

The Spy Who Loved Me had a lot going on. A Lotus that turned into a submarine, nukes going off in the Pacific, Bond skiing off of cliffs, thousands of orange jump suits and a tanker that gobbles up submarines. It was perhaps Roger Moore's best performance ever, but with a wholly forgettable lead villain.

Supervillain Stromberg was so unremarkable that it led to a change in fortunes for one of the film's other characters. Jaws, the 7ft 2in giant with metal teeth, was due to be killed off when Bond dropped him into a tank of Tiger sharks. Test audiences reacted badly to this, so the villain had to survive; Jaws killing Jaws, as it were. As for the unfortunate shark (arguably the real star of the show), an 8ft clay model was made for the final tussle.

LICENCE TO KILL, 1989

This film is such a gorefest that the shark scenes feel pretty tame. Alongside the deaths by heart removal, impaling by forklift, being harpooned, being fed into a heroin shredder, and being blown apart in a ruptured compression chamber, the shark deaths fall by the wayside. A more memorable death may be the security guard who fell into a tank with an Electric eel, resulting in a comedy lightshow.

Still, there are sharks in it. Superb shapeshifting sharks that seem to transcend species. In a scene where CIA agent Felix Leiter is lowered into a shark tank, we're led to believe that the beast inside is a Great white. Then we get an underwater shot of what looks like another Tiger shark — we can only assume that Eon Productions, which makes all the Bond films, has a Tiger shark account somewhere — before we get an animatronic head of a Great white.

Sadly, we've had no more shark-wielding Bond villains in the 32 years since that was made.

WARHEAD, 19??

Warhead is the Bond film that was never made, but was co-written by Sean Connery. Frankly, it would have been great too. They were looking at getting Alfred Hitchcock to direct it, with Richard Burton — Richard Burton! — to play the lead role of Bond. They even had eyes on Orson Welles to play Blofeld.

The plot? This is beautiful. First of all, Russian and American bombers are lured to the Bermuda Triangle so that the bad guys can steal their nuclear payloads. How to then take over the world with this freshly heisted arsenal? Remote-controlled robotic Hammerheads, each with a nuclear warhead for a bonce, sent up the sewers to detonate beneath cities, that's how. Apparently, the film was to wind up with Bond deactivating one of these sharks underneath Manhattan. Pure genius. It's a cinematic crime that this was never made. ∎

Left: *Richard Kiel as Jaws in The Spy Who Loved Me.*

Below: *Shark handlers on the set of Thunderball.*

Image: AF Archive /Alamy

British sharks

are (largely) cooler than you expect.

There's more to the UK coastline than cod, rain and disappointment. There's a whole ocean of predators out there, and many of them come a lot closer to our shores than you might expect.

Nathan Hill | Journalist

SHARKS. YOU already have the mental image. Organic grey submarines, fat as a sausage and bristling with teeth. The dead stare, menacing posture, triangular fins triangulating, stalking terrified divers in cages, a sawtooth of flesh breaking the surface. The seas around Britain are packed with sharks, over 10 million of the things. It's just that a lot of them don't look the part. Instead of the majestic man-eaters we've come to respect from iconic movies like Jaws and Sharknado, the British delegation is decidedly meek. Lithe and narrow, usually quite sedentary, and often with a fondness for deeper, cooler real estate, you'd be forgiven for never seeing one.

If we expand the range of British waters to include our portion of the Northeast Atlantic then we can claim ownership of over 40 shark species. Of these it's a roughly 50/50 split between the 21 that are permanent residents, and the 20 or so that just pass through. Spoiler: most of the exciting ones are occasional visitors.

I'll cut to the chase. A lot of the resident species are duller than the muddied British seas they live in. Dull to the point that even the fish and chip shops have to pitch them under inventive names to sell them. Huss? That's a shark, specifically a Nursehound, *Scyliorhinus stellaris*. Rock salmon or Sweet William? That's a Dogfish, *Scyliorhinus canicula*. I've never understood the naming worry; both are delicious, both should sell on their own eating merits.

In case you're wondering, in the UK we've not had a single unprovoked shark attack since the mid-1800s, when records began. Unfortunately, there doesn't seem to be a clear definition of what provocation of a shark is, so technically it could be anything from slightly spooking one to shoving a fist down its throat. What we can take away from this is that if you're floating on a lilo off of Bognor Regis, your chances of being bitten are pretty much zero.

Opposite page: *A Dogfish, Scyliorhinus canicula, inside its egg.*

Image: Nature Photographers Ltd / Alamy ➜

Image: Nature Picture Library / Alamy

Dogfish,
Scyliorhinus canicula

Maximum size: 85cm
Lifespan: approx. 20 years
Diet: Crustaceans, small fish, molluscs, worms and squid

Growing up on a seafront along the south coast, my childhood was decorated by Dogfish. Their corpses littered the beaches of my hometown, and occasionally the local commercial fisherman, tired of my nerdy ass watching them sorting through their catches on shore, would gift me a barely-living specimen fresh from the nets just to get rid of me. I'd skulk off, squatting like a Bedouin as I nurtured it in a tidal pool. Then it would die.

As a tourist at the seaside, it's one of the only British sharks you're likely to stumble upon alive, trapped in a rockpool, or simply washed ashore and exhausted after a brutal storm. A word of caution. If you ever find a moving Dogfish, don't grab it. It's unlikely to bite, but it'll wrap around you like a python and writhe, its abrasive sandpaper skin giving you a Chinese burn you'll never forget.

Likelier is that you'll find an egg. The Mermaid's purse, a long and leathery rectangular pouch that can be collected at the high tide mark amongst seaweed and shells, is the product of a Dogfish or one of its close cousins. Usually it'll be empty, but not always. Tightly sealed and waterproof until the young shark is ready to emerge, you might find one with the developing Dogfish embryo wriggling inside. Be a darling and pop it back in the sea if you do.

Angelshark,
Squatina squatina

Maximum size: 2.4m (females), 1.8m (males)
Lifespan: approx. 35 years
Diet: Specialises in eating flatfish but will take any other fish that ventures into the strike area, including rays

Maybe the least sharky of all is this wide, guitar-shaped lummox that looks like its mother had a fling with a stingray. It's flat, it's wide, it's brown and sandy, it lives on the sea floor and you'll probably never see one. Because we overfished them.

I've seen one. We used to keep it at the public aquarium I worked at, many years prior to 2010, when it was classified as Critically Endangered. In a tank measuring maybe 8x8m, filled with rays and crushed cockleshell for substrate, it would take several minutes just to find the thing, the camouflage was that good. It didn't even betray its position by breathing, having special accessory gill flaps underneath the body, expressly for the purpose of enhanced concealment.

It's an ambush predator through and through, and one that uses negative pressure to catch a meal. Prey swims overhead and the shark suddenly lunges upwards, the huge white mouth distending and sucking the victim in before it can even register it has been eaten. When feeding our captive Angelshark whole Mackerel on a pole, I found that moving the bait from the shark's tail to its snout elicited the best response, perhaps a behaviour that's reflected in the wild. But what stuck with me most was the sound. A low, almost subsonic concussion, like punching a side of beef, would always accompany the strike.

Image: Iophius_sub / Alamy

Greenland shark,
Somniosus microcephalus

Maximum size: potentially 7.3m
Lifespan: 270+ years
Diet: Fish, crustaceans, squid, some mammals

Depending on which measurements you want to use, the Greenland shark is up there as one of the largest meat eaters, rivalling the Great White. The Greenland has the potential to reach 7.3m long and a weigh up to a ton. It's also long-lived, something that mainstream media is always quick to blow out of proportion. Radiocarbon dating has reliably aged an individual to at least 272 years old, but that didn't stop journalists falling back on estimates and error bars to assign the Greenland a much more clickworthy lifespan of over 500 years. In the words of the scientist who led the research to ascertain the

shark's age: "Jesus Christ, why do they write this?" Either way, 272 years is still enough to make it the oldest living vertebrate on the planet.

You won't meet one in person. It lives as deep as 2,200m, and only comes up to the coldest of shallower waters — it's comfiest below 5°C, and if you're out swimming in that you're braver than me. It plays an important role as an apex predator in the Arctic where it eats seals and fish, though the remains of polar bears have been found inside some. Polar bear apologists will claim these must have already been dead when they were eaten, but that's what you would say if you were a bear fanboy.

The flesh of the Greenland shark is toxic unless treated. To make it edible the carcass is buried in gravelly sand and left for up to a year. Then the flesh is cut up and hung for several more months before being packaged and sold as Hakarl.

Frilled shark,
Chlamydoselachus anguineus

Maximum size: 1.96m
Lifespan: Estimated at 25 years
Diet: Smaller sharks, fish and squid

Where do we even start with the Godforsaken, antediluvian nightmare that is the Frilled shark? The teeth could be a good entry point (ironic if you're one of its prey items) with some 300 of the things, set in up to 29 rows, needle sharp and each with three jagged tips. There are so many teeth that they almost spill out of the mouth altogether, in a wide and macabre grimace, but that makes the shark all the better at grabbing and holding squid in the dark.

The name comes from the breathing apparatus — the gills make the Frilled shark and frills make the gills, in a glorious fleshy ruff.

If it looks ancient, that's because it's a living fossil; the anatomy of the Frilled shark can be found in fossil form as far back as some 95 million years.

Much like the Greenland shark, it's doubtful you'll ever meet one — it prefers cooler, deeper waters, though it will come up to the surface during the dead of night to feed, as long as it's cold enough.

Aside from being so damned ugly, its other claim to fame is a long gestation period. The female carries eggs that hatch internally (this is pretty common for sharks) and then she gives birth to 2-15 live pups. It's just that it can take her up to three and a half years before she actually delivers them.

→

Image: Paulo Oliveira / Alamy

Basking shark,
Cetorhinus maximus

Maximum size: 12m
Lifespan: approx. 50 years
Diet: Plankton, often copepod based

A fish so big that it doesn't even care what's in its way, happily ploughing into fishing boats and damaging itself in the process. It's a gentle but clumsy giant.

The risk is magnified in summer, when the upper layers of the sea are filled with the nutritious plankton that it feeds on. Of course, that also means that there's a chance — a slim chance — that you might see one in the flesh. I've seen one whilst stood on the beach in Hastings, apparently alongside half the town for company, with the shark swimming a dozen or so metres away from a shore pixelated with brown and grey shingle. It was an impressive presence, the shark becoming its own shadow, more a terrifying grey spectre than a clear physical mass, moving with a slow deliberation. Then its dorsal fin broke through the waves and everyone squealed.

Basking sharks are often presented as languid, but they can also breach the water, leaping clear of the surface before crashing back down. Why they do it is a mystery, but whatever the reason, we know that they reach around 18kph — twice the top speed of an Olympic swimmer — and jump to about 1.2m high.

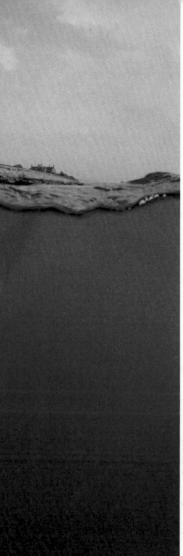

Tope,
Galeorhinus galeus

Maximum size: 1.95m (females), 1.75m (males)
Lifespan: approx. 50 years
Diet: Fish, squid, smaller sharks and rays

I saw a man catch one of these from a beach cast once. He was the sea-beaten stuff of legends, built like an ox, huge beard, haggard beyond his years; a true product of coastal gales and briny rain. To date, I've never heard anywhere swear as much as he did, hauling in that shark. Apparently, it was like trying to pull a car up the beach, and I've no reason to doubt him. Whoever made the rod deserves a knighthood.

The fish he pulled from the water lacked grace. Underwater, these are sleek creatures, about the length of an adult human but a whole lot stronger. In his arms, it just went limp, resigned to its demise. The fisherman returned it without even posing for a photo first.

The Tope is a protected species that can be found anywhere off of Britain pretty much all year round. If you want to spot one, your best bet is to look in an estuary somewhere — pregnant females come inshore to give birth, producing 20-30 pups at a time.

Throughout its lifetime the Tope can migrate terrific distances. Sharks tagged in British waters have later turned up in the Canary Isles, a trip of about 1500 miles.

→

Image: Minden Pictures / Alamy

Thresher shark,
Alopias vulpinus

Maximum size: around 6m, half being the tail
Lifespan: approx. 40 years
Diet: Schooling forage fishes such as sardines, squid and some crustaceans

With a face sketched in existential dread, the Thresher shark is a fish that looks exactly how I feel day to day.

The big problem with being an ocean-going shark is that your pelagic prey has an effective way of not being eaten — tighten up into a bait ball when there's a threat, then scatter in all directions when that threat tries to strike. It's a big ask to stay focused on one fish amongst a few thousand all going different ways.

The solution? A tail weaponised for whipping. I'm not talking 'glance the ball of fish with the tail on the way past' whipping. No, it's a full-frontal attack with the long lobe lashed directly over the head at the last moment. Speed is paramount, and the tail travels around 30mph into the shoal, enough to potentially cause cavitation of the water, sending out a localised shockwave to stun fish that aren't directly hit. One account records a tail striking at 80mph. Once whipped, the prey fish make for easy eating. That's why the tail accounts for half of the shark's length.

The other neat thing with a Thresher is that it warms its own blood, as several of the active hunting sharks do. The heating is only slight, giving it a body temperature some 2°C warmer than the surrounding water, but that's enough to improve muscle efficiency considerably.

Blue shark, *Prionace glauca*

Maximum size: 3.8m
Lifespan: approx. 20 years
Diet: Squid, fish, seabirds, dead mammals, smaller sharks

Two words: rough sex. The reproduction of Blue sharks is such a hostile affair that the female has had to evolve a toughened hide to deal with it. Her skin is three times thicker than that of the male.

Technically, it's a killer, but only if I stretch the timelines enough. From the late 1500s to now, we know of some 13 attacks on humans globally by Blue sharks, four of which turned out to be fatal. This one is a periodic visitor with a long migratory route, but it can be found seasonally off of any coast around Britain. Of all the sharks around our shores, this is up there are the most sharky of all. Long and powerful, with that gorgeous countershading — dark on top, light on the belly — to help it stay concealed.

Oddly, Blue sharks have a real issue identifying smooth surfaces, which is why they've always been such failures in captivity. Give them a rocky outcrop and they can spot it and avoid it. Give them a huge pane of aquarium glass and they'll just faceplant straight into it.

Great white shark?
Carcharodon carcharias

Maximum size: 6.1m (females), 4m (males)
Lifespan: approx. 70 years
Diet: Fish, sharks, seals, dolphins, porpoises, seabirds, turtles, even whales

What of the most revered shark of all? Is it here?

The press loves speculation about Great whites entering British waters, and not without good reason as claimed sightings are steadily growing.

Even though the nearest confirmed Great white we've ever had was back in 1977, nearly 170 miles off of Cornwall, the conditions closer to home 40+ years later are all the more favourable for them. Global rises in temperature mean that British waters spend longer within the 12-24°C range that Great whites prefer. We have an abundance of their favourite food items here, with all eyes on Orkney's huge seal populations, the largest colony of seals in Europe. Tuna visits are ever more common too, another Great white staple.

In recent times, one of our most credible sightings comes from just off of the Summer Isles, in the Highland region of Scotland. A small group of divers, and amongst them trained marine biologist Simon Greenstreet, spotted what they thought was a Basking shark on the surface of the water. Firing up their boat to go investigate, the shark turned aggressively towards them, coming at them in a way that Basking sharks don't. It swam alongside them for a while, giving Simon enough time to appraise the key markers: large and firm dorsal fin, pointed snout, small eyes set either side and distinct countershading of grey top/white underside.

The jury is out, but the consensus of experts is 'probably'. Remember, the oceans have no doors. ∎

Image: Wildestanimal / Alamy

PRACTICAL Fishkeeping

TRIAL OFFER: 3 ISSUES £3

Join a community of thousands of fishkeeping fanatics

Subscribe to Britain's best-selling fishkeeping publication and receive monthly inspiration and advice from the industry experts. Every issue also includes in-depth species showcases, incredible features on habitats from around the world and reviews of the latest available products.

Image: Marko Steffensen / Alamy

What happened to Meg?

The Megalodon was the largest predatory fish that lived, but sometimes being big just isn't enough.

Dr Neale Monks | Palaeontologist

WHETHER IT'S *River Monsters* or *Jaws*, giant predatory fish rarely fail to make an impression, perhaps because we instinctively feel so vulnerable when swimming through deep or murky waters. But of all the many aquatic giants that have ever lived, which was the biggest?

Perhaps surprisingly, my encounter with this leviathan of fishes was at that heartland of the 'Costa Geriatrica' — Eastbourne. At the tail end of the 1990s, I was part of a team studying how marine communities changed through the Late Cretaceous. This involved going to places like the chalk cliffs at Beachy Head to collect fossils, and these included lots of sharks' teeth. Among these were teeth assigned to a species called *Cretoxyrhina mantelli*. While this name might be unfamiliar, its ecological niche certainly won't be. This was a big mackerel shark, potentially 8m long, and similar to the modern Great white shark.

We'd also come across specimens of another shark species, *Cretalamna appendiculata*. It was

particularly voluminous animals, which placed them squarely on the menu as far as *Otodus* was concerned. *Otodus'* large size and robust teeth seem to have been adaptations for this particular niche, hungry sharks attacking small and medium sized whales from underneath, biting straight through the bones, before turning around to finish off their now fatally injured prey.

The Miocene (23-5 million years ago) was the heyday of the *Otodus* sharks, with plenty of small whales to eat, but towards the end of the Miocene life began to get tougher for these enormous predators. Remember how the mosasaurs caused problems for *Cretoxyrhina* back in the Cretaceous? History seems to have repeated itself, with big predatory whales — what would become the modern-day Sperm whales and Killer whales — increasingly competing with *Otodus* for food. And again, as with the more ecological flexible *Cretalamna* buzzing around the edges of the *Cretoxyrhina* 'giant shark' niche, there was the Great white shark, *Carcharodon carcharias*, waiting in the wings. Being that bit smaller, perhaps it could avoid direct competition with the large predatory whales, while still being large enough to take down seals and sealions without much bother. With stiff competition from Great whites and Killer whales, the giant *Otodus* had nowhere to go.

Exactly why the Megalodon went extinct remains unclear, but the one thing geologists can confirm is that they are definitely dead and gone. *Otodus* fossils have been dated to the Pliocene, about 3.5-2.5 million years ago, but no younger fossils than these have been found. This isn't for want of looking — *Otodus* teeth are quite common and have been found all around the world, even from deep sea dredges. But Megalodon teeth younger than the Pliocene just aren't out there, whatever Hollywood might have you believe — and that, if you're a small whale minding your own business, is probably a good thing. ∎

Image: R Kawka / Alamy

not as big as *Cretoxyrhina*, at maybe 3m, but the evidence points to both being opportunistic predators consuming everything from squid to fish, and turtles to pterodactyls. As the Cretaceous wore on, *Cretoxyrhina* struggled to compete with the mosasaurs, marine reptiles similar to modern monitor lizards but much, much bigger. By contrast, *Cretalamna* seems to have gone from strength to strength, its smaller size perhaps making it more adaptable and able to feed on a wider range of prey.

By the end of the Cretaceous, about 65 million years ago, *Cretoxyrhina* was extinct, as were the mosasaurs, but *Cretalamna* had morphed into another lineage of sharks: *Otodus*. This genus of sharks included several massive species that filled the apex predator niches no longer occupied by the giant sharks and marine reptiles of the Cretaceous. The biggest of these is the notorious Megalodon shark, *Otodus megalodon*. With an estimated maximum length of well over 12m, 'Meg' was easily the biggest predatory fish to have ever lived. Among extant fish, only the Whale shark and Basking shark are bigger. The Great white shark, with a paltry 6m to its name, is almost a minnow in comparison.

As this new geological age wore on, another group of animals were making their presence known: the cetaceans. Improbably derived from hoofed mammals, the early whales were initially not

Above: Otodus sharks with a modern diver for comparison.

Otodus megalodon (rear) was the largest macropredatory shark that ever lived. Males are assumed to have reached some 10-14m fully grown, with a weight of up to 34 tonnes. Females were larger, at a potential 13-17m fully grown, with a weight of up to 60 tones.

Otodus obliquus (front) lived around some 40-60 million years ago, and was the ancestor to the Megalodon. Despite not having the bulk of the Megalodon, it still measured a hefty 9-10m fully grown, weighing around 15 tonnes.

The diver is nervous.

Big Red

The mighty Pirarucu of South America faces a conservation crisis in real time. Farming presents an option to save wild stocks, but much work is still to be done to save this magnificent giant of the Amazon.

Max Pedley | Ornamental Aquatics Wholesale

The heart of the Amazon. Avian choirs chatter in a canopy of towering trees, standing guard over an empire of stagnation. A monster fierce, decorated in the finest armour of the Neotropics. Liveries of scarlet marking a beast set for war. The Red Fish. Alas, mankind sends deep the roots of exploitation and destruction. This is a war not even a living demon could win.

As myth would have it, Pirarucu, the son of a village chief, was struck by a storm fashioned by the hands of deities, casting him deep into the Tocantins river. Tupa, the God of Gods thought this punishment to be mild and so disincarnated him into the form of the Arapaima, forever to haunt the river. Such deeds were forced by his heathenly actions.

This demon fish of the rainforest has been said to have swallowed children whole, murdered fishermen mercilessly and capsized canoes with immense power. Given that lengths of 3 metres and weights of 200KG are not unheard of, such proposals seem not preposterous.

Left: *A licensed fisherman clubs a Pirarucu caught at the water's surface. Clubbing is a common method of dispatch for this giant fish.*

THE PIRARUCU, *Arapaima gigas*, is a big fish; the largest of the five species in the *Arapaima* genus. The name is a Portuguese derivation of local terms from the Tupi language — 'pira ucurum' translates across as 'red fish', a testament to the intense crimson flanks of the adults. Records show an average lifespan of 15-20 years in captivity, and akin to trees the Pirarucu can be aged by growth rings in its magnificent scales. Few reach that age.

The water level of the Amazon basin rises between December and April as the wet season transpires, and rivers, lakes and lagoons burst and spill as the rain beats down on the land. Water is the blood of the Amazon, flowing deep into the flooded forest, and the Pirarucu obligingly follow, seeking a spawning site. Shallow areas are preferred, where a spawning pit is dug by the parents, a furrow some 70cm long and 25cm deep. The breeding process is often misunderstood and unfairly compared to its close relative — we know much more about the spawning habits of their smaller cousins, the Arowana, a group of fish revered amongst aquarium fanatics. Arowana are easy fish to harvest. They are mouthbrooders, a strategy of reproduction that does what it says on the tin — eggs are picked up and carried in a special cavity in the throat, and retained there until the young are developed enough to fend for themselves. A collector only has to price the Arowana's jaws apart to reach their bounty.

Unlike the Arowana, the Pirarucu is not a mouthbrooder. The male may hurriedly resort to carrying the young briefly in his mouth, ferried from one location to another if the risk of predation becomes too great, but there's no real oral incubation. Instead, both parents guard the eggs and fry within their nest for several weeks until independence is reached. During this time, the parents fend off attacks from would be predators.

Unfortunately for the Pirarucu, a whole half decade is needed until they reach sexual maturity, but the fish becomes a target long before then. The mild, boneless flesh of Pirarucu is considered a delicacy by some, and a cheap surrogate for other fish by others — *Arapaima* is sold as a cheap alternative to Halibut in the United States.

Because of such palatability, individuals are lucky to reach five years of age before being harvested for the plate, though government mandated minimum catch sizes help to keep this in check, for licensed fishermen, at least. Their flavour is their demise, contributing to a diminishing population.

From 1996 to 1999, *Arapaima* fishing was outright banned across Brazil, which led to a huge recovery of stocks, but in recent times unregulated fishing may be once again dealing a sucker punch on what have become fragile, fragmented populations. Hunters harpoon, bludgeon and net fish in the dry season with ease, as they congregate in the receding waters. Three of the five described species have not been seen in tens of years, leading researchers to fear the worst. Yet the fish's plight still fails to capture the public imagination in the same was as seal or whale culling does elsewhere in the world.

On the face of it, returning to a total ban on the killing of *Arapaima* might seem like the obvious way to preserve what remains of the species, but the nature of South America's people, economy and politics makes this challenging. Many tribes receive sustenance from the fish, an important source of dietary protein, and policing unscrupulous fishermen in the deepest rural zones is near impossible. And what of alternative sources

Image: Reuters / Alamy

Left: Villagers of the Ramao Island community sit for a meal of Pirarucu after a day of fishing.

Right: Pirarucu, the 'Red fish', Arapaima gigas.

Image: Amazon-Images / Alamy

ISSUE 1 | 63

of income for the indigenous people, should the trade in *Arapaima* dry up? Palm oil plantations, cattle ranches, even cocaine; all are amongst the viable and profitable alternatives.

With that in mind it may seem somewhat perverse that I might suggest that more commercial farming — right there in the heart of the Amazon — can be of a benefit to native flora and fauna. Done correctly, farming can be as protective as it is productive. Ecologically merciless slash and burn programs for cattle ranches or monotonous and sterile palm oil plantations, all fuelled by the greed and need of the Western World, may be the only options available to a local trying to cut a living. Yet farming need not be quite so hopeless. *Arapaima gigas* inadvertently presents its head on a plate to humanity, a sacrificial Messiah for many species of the Amazon.

The benefits to farming Pirarucu are plain and obvious to the farmer. For one, the fish can thrive where other species would perish. *Arapaima* are obligate air breathers, forced to come to the water's surface every 10 to 20 minutes, where they gulp air

Above: Arapaima on sale at Manaus City Market, Brazil.

into a primordial lung — actually an adapted and high vascularised swim bladder. The 'coughing' of Pirarucu gasping at the surface is a common sound wherever they can be found, a convenient way for hunters to locate their prey. This oxygen exploiting hardware allows the fish to be farmed in huge densities, far higher than those of other commercially reared fish, in low-tech ponds as well as in low cost, non-invasive, DIY cages along rivers.

As well as their ability to cope with dense stocking, they have other merits. They are disease resistant and hardy. They can be grown quickly and reliably on poor quality foods, including low grade poultry, viscera, dead fish, proprietary pellets and even fruits. They lend themselves well to integrated aquaculture, whereby no product should be considered waste. The ammonia expelled as a part of the Pirarucu's basic biology is naturally refined and gives sustenance to plankton and algae, which in turn feeds forage fish and fry. Alternatively, fish kept in recirculating systems provide fertiliser for local plantations, benefiting the growth of crops.

A two-and-a-half-acre area dedicated to farming produces up to 600kg of *Arapaima* in a year, with each fish able to amass up to 15kg every twelve months. Working on local rates, $3000 revenue for this harvest can be achieved, with overheads kept to a minimum — especially where fish are kept in homemade pens on the main bodies of the river. The same area of land can bring a $4200 return if used to grown palm oil, but the overheads for this are greater. Machinery and other agricultural hardware present a significant investment of capital, as well as time taken for palms to grow. Environmentally speaking, there's no argument between the two. Two and a half acres of untouched Amazon forest can hold over 1500 species of plants, supporting the basis for an ecosystem. Remove it and a whole trophic chain of birds, primates, frogs and reptiles are all homeless. A cattle rancher will see an investment return of just $60 in that much space.

When I say nothing is considered waste, I mean it. The tongues of Pirarucu are used to grate berries, savoured by local tribespeople, or mixed with guarana bark to make a medicine, whilst the skin can be tanned and treated, crafting a leather more durable and flexible than that of cattle. Even the scales are amazing. Possibly the toughest, most flexible scales of any animal and impervious to

Right: A stipped Arapaima skin awaits processing, possibly to be tanned into leather.

Image: Minden Pictures, Alamy

attacks from Piranha, they spark 'bioinspiration' for use as battlefield armour and even aerospace design when they're not snapped up for use as nail files.

Perhaps with more research and investigation, the *Arapaima* has the potential to become a commercial gargantuan in the Amazon. We're now living in our own science fiction future, and it's entirely reasonable to think that domesticated, line-bred forms could be created to produce higher yields over a shorter timescale, reducing demand for the unregulated slaughter of wild fish.

As humanity transitions from survival to pleasure, so too do the uses of *Arapaima*. European anglers traverse Asia to reel in the largest of freshwater species in specially stocked lakes. There, imported and artificially introduced Pirarucu feature heavily, revered by the fishermen looking for the strongest sport — lived experience, a photo or two, and perhaps some bragging rights.

Mike Bailey of Exotic Fishing Thailand reports that almost all of his guests — over 90% as polled — visit with the aim of catching one of 100 Arapaima stocked in Mike's 10-acre lake. The fish cohabitate the water with other 'monster' fish, including two Critically Endangered species, Mekong Giant Catfish and Siamese Giant Barb, (*Pangasianodon gigas* and *Catlocarpio siamensis*, respectively) but rarely show aggression. As a matter of fact, Mike reports that they feed with an inhaling motion, seldom eating any species above 500g.

Nonetheless, how does such a financial gain from the fish bode for them in their native habitat? Minimally, it would seem. Ex-situ breeding seems relatively commonplace in artificial and isolated ponds through South East Asia, where they are bred for both sport and the ornamental aquaculture industry, though prices remain high. A quality 50KG specimen can fetch up to $2000 according to Mike, with as many as 80 of his total count weighing in at over 80KG. With this much bulk, the marketability of the fish for angling tourists shields it from ending up on the dinner table.

It's difficult to say how sport fishing could help the Pirarucu in its native range, though surely relieving the small stresses of sport fishing on wild fish is a benefit, even if only minor. One might even think about the ponds as resources for raising awareness for the fish, too.

On the face of it, the fish is an unrelenting super predator of the highest stature, the King of the Amazon. Underneath that literal hard outer shell,

a caring parent. A steward of the water, protective but not aggressive. Canoe capsizer? I guess it's possible. Fishermen killer? Possibly, with the thick, hard skull and powerful body, being struck by the tail could easily slap an unwary handler insensible, to sink down unconscious and drown beneath the water. Child swallower? Probably not.

To consider it a devil, through ancient culture or otherwise, could be disingenuous. Consider it a survivor, doing what it must to ensure its genetics continue, the same as all life on Earth. It's just unfortunate that having millions of years to evolve its natural defences, these turn out to be powerless against the onslaught of humanity. Ironically, its unique air breathing capability, along with its ability to amass so much edible flesh each year, might turn out to be the traits that prompt humans to care for it the most.

Surrendering its evolutionary adaptations to serve us and our demands, could this fish, so seemingly set for battle, really be a prisoner of war? Providing its produce for us, may Pirarucu undo his evil deeds of the past and succour the Amazon rainforest and all which resides within? Let's hope. ■

Below: The flesh of Pirarucu is hung and dried in the sun before being salted.

Right: A single huge scale, prized amongst local people as a nail file.

Image: Minden Pictures, Alamy

Image: Minden Pictures, Alamy

PIRARUCU / ARAPAIMA GIGAS

The Pirarucu occurs across South America in Brazil, Colombia, Guyana and Peru, but it also found in Bolivia where it is thought to have escaped from a Peruvian farm during a flood before becoming an invasive species.

It's an obligatory air breather, only able to spend some 5-20 minutes underwater at a time before returning to the surface. Denied this, it will drown.

The typical size for an adult is around 200cm, which can weigh in at up to 200kg. There are some unverified records of Pirarucu reaching 450cm, with 300cm being confirmed.

The fish is a living fossil, evolutionarily unchanged for some 23 million years, and its ancestry can be traced back to Gondwanaland, the prehistoric supercontinent that went on to split into South America, Africa, Madagascar, Arabia, Sri Lanka, India, Australia and Antarctica.

In the wild the Pirarucu mainly eats fish, but will take fruits and seeds as well. On occasions is has been observed leaping clear of water to snatch reptiles, birds and primates from overhanging branches.

Arapaima is an important food fish, referred to locally as the 'Cod of the Amazon'. The flesh is typically salted and dried, meaning it can be stored without refrigeration, an important consideration for life deep in the rainforest.

The Exocet

Kenton Geer | Vicious Cycle Fisheries

I DO NOT envy the Flying fish. Although arguably the most gifted of all Mother Nature's aquatic species, it is also the most agonised creature in the world's oceans.

Its gifts are equally a blessing and a curse. God gave the Flying fish the natural abilities that man has envied since time immemorial—a dual capacity to both soar freely through the air and breathe underwater. Yet it's this skillset that leaves it at a constant unrelenting attack both above and below the water line.

When a Flying fish isn't being chased by a larger predatory fish, it takes its chances skyward, only to be chased by a predatory bird. Sometimes the more God-gifted abilities we are given, the more pressure we receive in return from the outside.

I have never had a good personal relationship with Flying fish. Although I can appreciate their plight, their attraction to the bright lights of fishing boats often leads them to the same demise that the lights of the city curse upon landed sailors. They come recklessly flying in only to never leave again. Dead Flying fish often cover the bow of a boat like the drunkards that line Bourbon Street.

Flying fish have broken my sunglasses straight off my face and have hit me so many times on deck I've lost count. They have violently awoken me in my bunk, having glided into the cabin at the most unlikely of angles.

I've even had a giant Flying fish hit the end of my penis so hard one night while I hung it over the side to urinate that I contemplated cancelling the whole trip and taking the boat back to shore to get medical help for the swelling.

Opposite page: *Like a fish out of water.*

Saving Lau'ipala

In a war of legislation between activists and industry, the voices of indigenous communities have become collateral damage, overshadowed by bluster and posturing. Marine biologist Bryce Risley navigates a complex battlefield to find the true victims.

Bryce Risley | Marine Social Ecologist

I DEVELOPED A love for aquatic life at an early age. That's nothing unusual for someone growing up near oceans, lakes, or rivers where you'll routinely chance upon some submerged and scaly life-form. Living by water often goes hand in hand with loving what's in the water.

But I didn't grow up near water. I grew up in the New Mexico desert, just over 1,000 km away from the nearest beach in Puerto Peñasco. I grew up in the driest state in America where — aside from the Rio Grande river, a handful of remote reservoirs, and the occasional dry creek — I was unlikely to encounter a fish in the wild. Then, in 1996, the City of Albuquerque opened the state's first public aquarium and I've been immersed in the life aquatic ever since. Fast forward to 2021 and I've attended domestic and international aquarium conferences, worked at fish stores and public aquariums, and spent three years researching aquarium industry supply chains in Sri Lanka for my graduate degree.

Being engaged with the aquatics industry for over 17 years, I'm amazed by how much it's grown.

The scene is alive with pioneering LED light designs, wavemaker pumps that recreate tidal action, the latest in aquarium automation tech, and, of course, the livestock that underpins it all. Aquarium livestock, both freshwater and marine, now carries an annual global turnover of some $5 billion, and in the US, roughly 20% of the aquarium trade consists of marine organisms. It's loosely estimated that 50 million marine animals — fish, corals and invertebrates — are caught and sold to hobbyists around the world every year.

To feed this industry, livestock must be caught or cultured. Breakthroughs in aquaculture are now commonplace as we learn new techniques for how to breed and rear many of the delicate fishes and corals aquarists love to keep. The media, and especially aquatic journalism, is quick to seize on these successes and give them the airtime they deserve.

Synchronously, there's a handful of less sensationalist industry topics that advance at a much slower pace, if they advance at all. We still can't consistently quantify or trace species collection

Image: Doug Perrine, Alamy

Yellow tangs clean a sea turtle.

volume in the marine aquarium trade, for example. Then there's the decades-old practice of cyanide fishing, even though it's less prevalent these days. This technique, which involves stunning wild fish with a sodium cyanide mixture in order to capture them, still happens in the Philippines and Indonesia (and possibly elsewhere), and always brings with it lethal consequences and environmental damage.

Within marine aquarium circles there's one topic which seems to frequently catch media interest, to the chagrin of anyone who follows it — Hawai'i.

For a story that's ever polarised and evolving, Hawai'i has it all: robust scientific data, misinformation campaigns, legal controversies, and an ongoing battle over resource rights, ethics, and conflicting value systems. There's one narrative in the Hawai'i saga which has been consistently absent from the ever-deepening pool of articles and content, and that's the Native Hawaiian perspective.

Aquarium collection of livestock in Hawai'i began in the 1970's, and has until recently supplied the multinational aquarium industry. Years of controversial legal debates have kept parties invested in the West Hawai'i Aquarium Fishery (WHAF) on edge, as aquarium fish collection has been consistently targeted and challenged by non-profit organisations in opposition to the aquarium industry. Special interest groups including For the Fishes, Earth First, the Conservation Council of Hawai'i, the Humane Society of the United States, and the Center for Biological Diversity began targeting the aquarium industry in Hawai'i some 40 years ago. These organisations mainly relied on outdated information to make the claim that overfishing was occurring, and cited grossly exaggerated fish mortality rates as reasons to shut down the fishery. Largely obscured by this — usually no more than a footnote to the conservation-focused arguments — another argument was made in defence of Native Hawaiian gathering rights and cultural considerations; an argument which addressed the fishery's incompatibilities with Hawaiian values.

The Hawai'i archipelago consists of six major islands including Kauai, Oahu, Molokai, Lanai, Maui, and Hawai'i, also referred to as the 'Big Island', and Native Hawaiians have traditionally fished around all for subsistence purposes.

This historic practice aligns with traditional Hawaiian conservation values, something reflected in passages from the Kumulipo, the Hawaiian creation chant where the ancient chief Maui is taught to fish using a hook and line. Customary Hawaiian fishing practices place management responsibilities in the hands of community members who practice gathering only what they need to feed their communities.

I spoke with several Native Hawaiians who shared their thoughts on how the practice of collecting wild fishes to keep in aquariums is not in alignment with the acceptable uses of Hawai'i's natural resources. "Hawaiians collect fish to eat, and if somebody else wants to take fish to eat, that's not in conflict with our culture. Take what you need to eat, we are happy to share. But aquarium fish collecting does not provide sustenance," says Charlie Young, a member of the West Hawai'i Fishery Council (WHFC).

In contrast to Western culture — which tends to value environmental resources in monetary terms — many Indigenous communities such as those in Hawai'i experience relationships with nature where

Below: *Charlie Young of the West Hawai'i Fishery Council.*

Image: ArteSub, Alamy

Above: *Yellow tangs are valuable controllers of algae.*

natural resources are not commodified and their use is not motivated by profit.

Native Hawaiian cultural practitioner Mike Nakachi shared his concerns over the WHAF and its incompatibilities with Hawaiian gathering practices.

"Here's the common question that we ask. Does aquarium fish collecting practice what our traditional customary practices called Malama Āina? Malama Āina means to take care of one's place. Take care of the Hawaiian Islands. Does this practice of extraction benefit the Hawaiian Islands? And I don't mean that from a monetary perspective," Nakachi remarks.

Fishes collected in Hawai'i have long been favoured by hobbyists and public aquariums alike. Prized for their abstract and beautiful coloration, unique morphologies and behaviours and even their endemism (exclusivity to a single geographic area) and rarity, it's easy to see why many aquarists are passionate about their hobby. One species in particular, the Yellow tang, *Zebrasoma flavescens*, hogs much of the attention in stories about the WHAF. Given its high demand, the vibrant yellow fish once accounted for 82% of the catch taken from the fishery, according to the Hawai'i Department of

Land and Natural Resources (DLNR), the governing body responsible for the management of the fishery.

The Yellow tang, named Lau'ipala (yellow leaf) by Native Hawaiians, is beloved by locals and tourists alike. It can be found schooling among near-shore reefs where the protruding sloped snout is used to graze algae. Contrasting the yellow body, there are white, retractable spines at the base of the tail which are used for defence, a weapon carried by all tangs. While the Yellow tang's range extends across the Pacific as far as Japan, no region boasts an abundance of the fish comparable to Hawai'i, making the remote archipelago ideal for their collection.

To catch Lau'ipala, the schooling fish are corralled into a barrier net, where they are hand sorted by size: juveniles are kept and mature individuals are released. Once divers have ascended with their catch, they board their collection vessel and proceed to delicately vent excess gas resulting from decompression from the fish's swim bladder using a hypodermic needle. This procedure, commonly referred to as fish venting or needling, is said to be similar to giving your pet a vaccine. Once vented, fish are placed in holding tanks while the collection vessel returns to shore to offload the catch.

→

Early in the fishery's history, reports of declining reef fish populations led to the passage of House Bill 3457, signed into law as Act 306 during the 1997-98 Hawai'i State Legislative Session. Act 306 called for the establishment of the West Hawai'i Regional Fishery Management Area (WHRFMA). Therein, Fish Replenishment Areas (FRAs) were implemented to conserve populations of fish targeted by aquarium collectors. The FRAs make up 35.2% of Hawai'i's 236km western coastline, extending from Ka Lae in the south to 'Upolo Point in the north. While seemingly large numbers of between 300,000 and 500,000 juvenile Yellow tangs were reportedly collected from the fishery each year, a 2020 report by the Hawai'i Department of Aquatic Resources (DAR) estimated overall populations of the fish at around 5.7 million individuals. Populations of Lau'ipala have increased 165% within the FRAs and 101% in the surrounding waters where aquarium fishing occurs. That's an increase of some 3.4 million fish, or 120% since the FRAs were established in December of 1999. Given the conclusions of well-documented studies on the WHRFMA, many marine scientists and proponents of the marine aquarium trade consider the WHAF the best managed near-shore coral reef fishery in the world.

While the replenishment areas have proven widely successful in conserving fish populations utilised by aquarium collectors, this is more a victory for industry, science, and management agencies than for Native Hawaiians. "In the process that we went through to establish the West Hawai'i Fishery Management Area, I cannot remember any Hawaiian being in favour of aquarium fish collecting except those who were directly benefiting from it by doing the diving and what have you. And that was all for profit," says Young.

It's important to note that while members of the Native Hawaiian community have been involved in conversations pertaining to the management of the fishery, it was through their own initiatives that their voices came to be heard. Dialogue was carried out through the West Hawai'i Fishery Council (WHFC) which Young has served on since its inception in June of 1998. The placement of the FRA's was determined by scientists and Native Hawaiian members of the WHFC so as to overlap and preserve traditional Hawaiian fishing grounds,

Right: *Yellow tangs as seen in shallow waters.*

Image: TMI, Alamy

Image: Imagebroker, Alamy

Above: As well as cleaning algae from rocks, Yellow tangs also stop it from choking light-hungry coral beds.

in addition to encompassing fish spawning locations and prominent reef formations. "At face value, the West Hawai'i Fishery Council was equitable because it included Native Hawaiians, but I think it doesn't call out the fact that Native Hawaiians had never been included before. Unless we had put our voice forward, it never would have happened. They didn't seek us out, we had to put ourselves in there." comments Young.

The DAR implemented a White List in 2013 to account the 40 species which could be legally collected from the fishery. Although the conservation statuses of species targeted by aquarium collectors suggest a responsibly managed fishery, Native Hawaiians have specific concerns about the collection of the Kole tang, *Ctenochaetus strigosus*, and Pāku'iku'I, or Achilles tang, *Acanthurus achilles*. As well as being in demand by the aquarium industry, both of these species are utilised as food throughout the Hawaiian Islands and at that time represented the second and third most collected species in the WHAF.

According to the 2019 NOAA Fisheries West Hawai'i Integrated Ecosystem Assessment,

non-commercial fishing including recreational, subsistence, and fishing for cultural purposes comprise the second largest fishery by weight in Hawai'i, while the pelagic (open ocean) commercial fishery which targets tuna and billfish is the largest. Overcollection of coral reef fish for food consumption has become a more serious concern for the state and Native Hawaiians alike. While nearly all of the coral reef fishes are consumed locally, many of the pelagic species fished from Hawai'i's waters are exported to distant markets.

Not all Hawaiians rely on fishing for subsistence to the same degree. Some may fish for themselves, their families, or their community only on occasion while others may have fish at their table every day of the week. Whether aquarium collection of these species negatively impacts food abundance for Native Hawaiians or not is not the principal concern of Hawaiians. The fundamental issue is a difference between Western and Indigenous relationships with the natural world.

Nakachi shared a brief story about the history of this relationship in Hawai'i. "There is traditional knowledge that goes back thousands of years to the

Kumolipo. It's a chant, something that has been passed on for hundreds of years, and one of the first verses of it goes back to the formation of a coral polyp. And from the first coral polyp creates the house of coral which then provides a home for fish. Part of that story is that almost anything, flora or fauna, are forms of *kinolau*, which is a being that would be a symbiont with the native people, Kānaka Maoli.

"You would not want to offend any of the *kinolau* without asking for permission. You would reverently say a prayer to ask for a bountiful harvest and try to go catch something to provide for your family. The Hawaiian way is we only try to catch what we need to eat to provide for our families," he recounts.

The opinions of Native Hawaiians who are not associated with the WHAF are as important as those of Young and Nakachi, who have spent decades defending their culture from intrusive Western practices. I spoke to professional surfer Cliff Kapono who has spent much of his life riding waves in Hawai'i and asked for his thoughts on aquarium fish collection.

"There are animals out there that need to be cared for and rehabilitated. Sharks that lose a fin, or turtles that were struck by a prop (boat propeller), whales who lost their pod. There's a way for us to help marine organisms get back to where they need to be, and if they can't be rehabilitated then there's a place for them. I can appreciate that role of an aquarium but taking a perfectly living small Yellow tang off of a reef where its ecological benefit is extremely high, it's not just damaging the reef, it's also damaging those who depend on that reef to survive," he says. Young and Nakachi echoed Kapono's sentiments, expressing that public aquariums can play important roles in the rehabilitation of marine life.

Following a resolution by the Hawai'i Supreme Court in September of 2017, it was determined that the Department of Land and Natural Resources (DLNR) is obligated to uphold an environmental review of the fishery in accordance with regulations set forth by the Hawai'i Environmental Policy Act (HEPA). This decision was the result of a legal case representing a number of environmental non-profits, and a collective of Native Hawaiians filed against the DLNR arguing that the fishery was subject to environmental review and that the agency had been permitting aquarium collection without procedural compliance. The HEPA process, HAR Chapter 11-200.1 dictates that an Environmental

Image: Roberto Nistri, Alamy

Impact Statement (EIS) must be completed to disclose environmental, economic, social, and cultural impacts resulting from a proposed activity that requires government permitting. The EIS was completed and submitted to the DLNR by the Pet Joint Advisory Council on April 23, 2020.

A month later, the Board of Land and Natural Resources (BLNR) cast a 7-0 vote, unanimously rejecting the EIS.

On June 25th, 2020, a collective of 21 scientists, all with PhDs, published an op-ed in West Hawai'i Today titled 'My Turn: We Expect Better', which chastised the BLNRs rejection of the Final

Above: The snout has evolved for a niche diet of greenery.

→

Environmental Impact Statement. The article's grievance focused solely on the BLNR's alleged dismissal of science. However, the statement did not address the agency's comments requesting additional information on other aspects of the fishery.

The BLNR detailed fourteen reasons for their non-acceptance of the EIS. Of importance in ensuring that Native Hawaiians are not overlooked in the assessment process is item 13 which notes a 'failure to sufficiently consider cultural impacts' stating that 'a number of testimonies expressed misgivings from a cultural standpoint with the proposed activity itself, regardless of impact on resources, and this was not adequately considered in concluding no significant impact.' Put another way, policy makers are obligated to consider factors beyond the data when making decisions. "Hawaiians by and large are purposely dismissed because they become an obstacle for the state to do its mandate," says Young.

Environmental law scholar Robin Craig who researches 'all things water', elaborated on why this tunnel vision on science-based decision making and data can be problematic. "Scientific studies that indicate a level of collection is sustainable barring massive changes from things like climate change may be accurate, but that information may not be answering the policy question that policy makers are most interested in answering. Getting scientists to grasp that is really hard," Craig says.

"Even when you have the scientific information, we have never lived in the United States, in a culture that was a scientocracy. There's no way you can allow science be the final arbiter of everything because the decision to let science decide is itself a value choice," she adds.

On January 12th, 2021, after years of legal disputes led by activist organised non-profits and a vocal group of Native Hawaiians, Hawai'i's First Circuit Court ruled that all Commercial Marine Licenses used in the WHAF would be suspended pending review, as a result of noncompliance with the HEPA.

So, why weren't the legal challenges regarding the WHAF's impacts on Native Hawaiian culture raised earlier in the fishery's history? Simply put, the political tools needed to advocate for Native Hawaiian rights were altogether absent at the time of the fishery's inception. Even today it remains up to Native Hawaiians to inform the state about

> ' The Yellow tang, named Lau'ipala (yellow leaf) by Native Hawaiians, is beloved by locals and tourists alike. It can be found schooling among near-shore reefs where the protruding sloped snout is used to graze algae '

their culture, and what types of practices are considered offensive to it. There are several key events and pieces of legislation which address the historic marginalisation of Native Hawaiians such as The Hawai'i Constitutional Convention of 1978 which resulted in the establishment of the Office of Hawaiian Affairs, a semi-autonomous 'self-governing body' which works to improve the well-being of Native Hawaiians.

United States Public Law 103-150, informally referred to as the Apology Resolution, was signed by congress in 1993 and serves to recognise the illegal overthrow of the Kingdom of Hawai'i at the hands of

United States troops in 1893. The bill communicates a commitment to 'provide a proper foundation for reconciliation between the United States and the Native Hawaiian people' while acknowledging 'Long range economic and social changes in Hawaii over the 19th and early 20th centuries have been devastating to the population and health and well-being of the Native Hawaiian population.'

As a researcher myself, I understand the frustration felt by scientists when their hard work doesn't become the vehicle of standardisation and progress they hope it will be. What is at stake for those in support of or in opposition to the WHAF are different things. The integrity of science and quality research is something we all stand to benefit from.

What are the implications of establishing policy when science is not the only consideration that decision makers are obligated to review? It depends on what's at stake, and that's almost always circumstantial. Fervent claims have been made by researchers and industry leaders that closure of the WHAF will set off a domino effect of marine aquarium fishery closures, ultimately leading to the destruction of the industry. Whether this speculation is realised or not remains to be seen.

Now is an opportune time to take a collective step back and reflect on a precedent that was set hundreds of years ago. In Hawai'i and across much of the world a precedent was set that to this day overlooks the voices of Indigenous peoples. The Hawai'i Environmental Policy Act is an essential piece of legislation that includes an effort to prevent further damage being done to Hawai'i's Native communities. I asked Young if he saw any room for compromise with the WHAF. "Compromise inherently means both sides get some part of what they want. The aquarium fish collectors have had what they've wanted for a long, long time with no benefit to Hawai'i. This would be a bad compromise for us. It would be a bad precedent to compromise with an activity which is in such disagreement with our culture," he says.

While science-informed decision making in policy will continue to prove essential to ensuring natural resources are sustained into the future, we must work harder to ensure the initiatives of science and industry remain equitable to all communities who stand to be influenced by them. By trying to dismiss key pieces of legislation such as the Hawai'i Environmental Policy Act which safeguards Native Hawaiians and their culture, researchers and industry leaders have missed an opportunity to start overdue conversations which might re-instil dignity, trust, and respect to Hawai'i's Native people.

"I'm not in disagreement with the science," Young says as he explains what motivates him to continue fighting to defend Native Hawaiian communities. "We're trying to recover from something. That's our goal, to recover from what occurred to us as a people years ago. This is about our culture, it's about our resources, it's about our land and who we are." ∎

Left: *Lau'ilapa's cultural importance is impossible to overstate.*

Image: Paulo Oliviera, Alamy

THANKS

I'm obliged to the many knowledgeable individuals who contributed to informing this article and my understanding of the highly complex dynamics surrounding the West Hawai'i Aquarium Fishery. While not all were mentioned by name, I express my thanks to Charlie Young, Robin Craig, Mike Nakachi, Cliff Kapono, David Sakoda, Bruce Carlson, Brian Tissot, Kevin Chang, and Kaimi Kaupiko.

A wee nibble

What are we supposed to make of the legend of
the fish that invades the human urethra?

Steve Grant | Amateur Ichthyologist

FEW FISHES are more mysterious or steeped in folklore than the Candirú. Here we have a catfish that has allegedly entered into the ears, noses, penises, vaginas and anuses of humans bathing or relieving themselves in South American freshwaters. There was even a nineteenth century written account of a French naturalist being told by fishermen that if one stood outside of the water but urinated in it, the catfish would launch out of the water and swim up the column of urine and into the urethra. Madness.

The earliest publication on Candirú invading humans dates back to 1829 and since then there have been numerous articles, TV programmes and even books devoted to the subject. Most people think this is a fallacy (or maybe phallusy), but some of the accounts appear to be clearly made. Most of those tend to relate to vaginal Candirú penetrations, the fish allegedly attracted by the menstrual blood.

Before the general availability of fitted underwear, river dwellers and fishermen used to wear sheaths to protect their genitals. These sheaths possessed small apertures or long tubes to allow them to urinate. The threat, perceived or otherwise, was taken seriously, though some say that the penis sheaths were possibly used to protect from equally worrying piranha bites. The current medical view is that whilst there may have been a small number of accidental penetrations into the lower orifices of humans, the traumatogenic risk is extremely low.

Let's clarify which fish we are discussing. In the order of catfishes, known as the Siluriformes, there is a family known as the Trichomycteridae, often called Pencil or Parasitic catfishes, despite the fact that not all of them are actually parasitic. Within the family are eight subfamilies. In one of these, all of the members are parasitic, but also exclusively hematophagous, or blood eaters. These are the catfish of Vandelliinae. In this subfamily are four genera: *Vandellia*, which is the most famous and the one normally called Candirú, as well as *Paracanthopoma*, *Paravandellia*, and *Plectrochilus*.

Some of the scientific names (including the synonyms) for these catfishes allude to their alleged trophic ecology: *Branchioica* ominously means 'gill' and 'a place to live'. *Plectrochilus diabolicus* translates as 'spur lip' and 'devil'. *Urinophilus* means 'urine loving', while *sanguinea* reads as 'bloodthirsty'.

Translate the South American common names into English and there are further treats. One has the name of Lancet bloodsucker, or Son of Streaky catfish — this latter because when large catfish of the species *Pseudoplatystoma magdaleniatum* are pulled from the water, these small parasitic catfishes fall out of their gills.

That these fish exclusively eat blood is fascinating in itself but how they do it is equally fascinating.

> Before the general availability of fitted underwear, river dwellers and fishermen used to wear sheaths to protect their genitals

Opposite page: *A Candirú attacking the gills of a Black pacu.*

Image: Pally /Alamy

Some examples are:

Paravandellia oxyptera — A study in 1983 involved specimens of large *Pseudoplatystoma* catfish being tied up at the riverbank. Within four to ten minutes of the *Pseudoplatystoma* going near the river bank, hundreds to thousands of small parasitic catfish swam alongside them and entered the gills for one to three minutes, leaving with bloated bellies on exit. Some were also seen apparently rasping on the skin of the unfortunate study samples. A single *Pseudoplatystoma* could feed thousands of *Paravandellia*, sometimes over a period of six hours. It is likely that before the host species was present, the parasite catfish were concealed underneath the substrate, buried and waiting in the sand.

Vandellia — It appears that species of this genus also live in the sand, and a paper in 2004 found that they enter the gills of larger fish and seek out the major gill arteries. They anchor on to and bite these arteries, and the blood is presumably pumped into their gut by the hosts' blood pressure. The authors suggested that the parasites do not need any special sucking mechanism to fill their stomachs with blood but use their needle-like teeth to make an incision in an artery — a proposal that would make the term 'bloodsuckers' redundant for these fish. Another study in 2001 found that *Vandellia* did not respond to chemical attractants like ammonia, amino acids, fresh fish slime, and human urine. Instead, their interest was only aroused when they saw a live fish, which would seem to be the final word on any theory that suggests that Candirú are attracted to urine.

Paracanthopoma — In 2015 a study found a species of this genus riding the giant pimelodid catfish *Zungaro zungaro* in the upper Amazon. The parasites were found on the host's caudal (tail) and pectoral (side) fins, as well as on its body at the base of the dorsal (top) fin. They weren't just hanging on; they had their snouts buried up to the eyes in the tough skin of the catfish host. Other holes were also found on those areas, presumably where other

specimens had been. The conclusion was drawn that they probably still fed on the host fish's gills, but that were also hitching a ride on their meal provider.

Plectrochilus diabolicus — The type specimen of this species was found halfway buried in the belly of a large *Pseudoplaystoma* catfish. It had burrowed directly through the body-wall and was distended with blood. It is not clear if the blood was from the body of the host, or from a feed from elsewhere on the body/gills.

Whilst this hypothesis does not appear to have been proposed by scientists, it's my own opinion that the documented behaviour of *Paracanthopoma* and *Plectrochilus* could explain the accounts of Candirú burrowing into the orifices of humans.

> ❝ They anchor on to and bite the arteries, and the blood is presumably pumped into their gut by the hosts' blood pressure. ❞

To wit: if their natural behaviour is to do this to large catfishes, and that they find their prey through sight (and therefore possibly through movement) it isn't a stretch to see why they would sometimes mistake a human and their orifices for the holes in which some seem to temporarily reside.

A final interesting note about these parasitic catfish is their morphology, which as one would expect, has evolved in line with their ecological habits. They have claw like teeth on the upper jaw, presumably for slashing the artery; external teeth on the gill bones, presumably for holding on; an absence of functioning pharyngeal jaws (jaws that live in the throats of many fish), presumably because they are of no use for eating blood; digestive systems that can cope with large volumes of blood, including strange fat globules in the stomach; loss of pigment, presumably for going unseen when dug into their hosts or buried in the substrate; and elongated bodies — all the better to slither into gills.

But what of them attacking humans? While the few accounts of urethral invasion are as scarce as they are contentious, video did recently emerge of an unidentified Candirú species that had aggressively attached itself to the back of a hapless South American swimmer. The fish had a tremendous grip, leading the swimmer to bleed after it had been removed, and it was bloated with blood. Whether this was from a prior meal or from the swimmer's back was never established. ∎

Below:
Vandellia cirrhosa, the classic Candirú.

Image: Paulo Oliveira /Alamy

STINCKING HERRINGS

And why the English turn up their noses

Graeme Rigby | Rigby's Encyclopaedia of the Herring

Ash Wednesday, 1555. Somewhere in Europe.

Some beare about a herring on a staffe, and lowde doe rore,
Herrings, herrings, stincking herrings, puddings now no more.

Popish Kingdome, Thomas Naogeorgus, ('englyshed' by Barnabe Googe, 1570)

THE LOUD-ROARING herring-resenters were searching for their lost 'feastes'. Catholic Fast Days took up nearly half the eating week, plus Lent. Salted or highly salted and smoked red, the King of Fishes suffered through over-familiarity. Across Northern Europe The Reformation brought meal time freedom and most nations got over it. Not the English. The continent's culinary diversification is traced to The Reformation and from that table heaving with possibilities, England went for meat, preferably beef. Fish & chips might live in the hearts of the nation, but ideally fried in dripping.

Fried fish came with 16th century Sephardic Jewish refugees from Portugal. By the 19th century it was contributing to the herring's downfall as street food. Cod, just beginning to turn, could be sold off to the street fryers. Once herring turns, even batter won't help. But across Northern Europe it was salt herring which captured people's exploitable hearts.

Largely ignoring Anglo-Scottish protestations of sovereignty, the Dutch claimed the British coastline's vast shoals as Divine Providence and out of plenty they even contrived a delicacy in *maatjes* — sweet, fat virgin spawners.

Gutting and salting on their factory-ship herring busses, they also brought hoopla. Fast *ventjagers* (sale-hunters) raced home with the first maatjes barrels, a brand leader to capture inflated prices. The great Amsterdam surgeon Nicolaes Tulp wrote of the excitement inland, where *the brined herring is adorned with green garlands and brought to the crossroads to be displayed and ceremonially eaten.*

In *Medical Observations* (1641) Tulp records a pregnant woman craving salt herring so much she ate 1,400 of the things before coming to term. It's unlikely he would have observed such a thing in England, at a time where the product quality was notoriously unreliable.

Preferring the stick of law to the carrot of quality, in 1563 the English had introduced secular Fish Days. The Catholic-leaning Stuarts, obsessed with Dutch herring power, readily adopted the Elizabethan measures, enabling Fish Days to be seen as papist conspiracy. James II, dodgiest of the lot, had even been Governor of the Royal Fishery.

Towards the end of the 18th century the Scots cracked quality control. Helped by four Anglo-Dutch wars that had kept the opposition in port, Britain became top herring nation. By 1911 it was salting over 2,500,000 tonnes a year for Russia and Germany, but, by then, hardly any for the home market. After World War I, undercut by Norway and Iceland's purse seining fleets, the market for British salt herring collapsed. A 1937 parliamentary debate on the recently established Herring Industry Board saw a discussion on distributing the excess production to the poor. Walter Elliot, Minister for Scotland, was however clear, *You cannot feed necessitous children on raw salt herring. I can imagine nothing which would upset a child more.* Not even hunger.

The Herring Industry Board offered booklets with *Scores of Simple Recipes*, but even with Merle Oberon saying, *Aren't Herrings delicious?* on the cover, it didn't turn the tide. The only positive signs identified in 1937 were expanding markets in the USA and Palestine — and thereby hung another tale of Jewish refugees.

Prototype herring fish fingers were tried in the 1950s, but Britain's market testing housewives went for cod. North Sea population collapse brought the 1970s ban on herring fishing and, when they returned to the fishmongers' slabs, they simply had too many bones. And in the relentless rise of the middle class, their associations were with cheap food and the poor. Kippers had become breakfast treats, but good breakfasts were on their way out too. By 2013, England's major herring quota owners had sold nearly all of it to a single Dutch supertrawler.

Culinary times are changing. You can hardly move, these days, for celebrity chefs filleting mackerel, but who will sing the joys of the herring, the Silver Darling, the King of Fishes? ◼

Opposite page: *'Aren't herrings delicious?'* asks an ambitious Merle Oberon.

Below: *By the 1960s, the Herring Industry Board was moving away from using fish images in its advertising.*

Glowing Vitality - comes from Herring

Cut down on housekeeping bills and at the same time build up your family's health. Give them plenty of tasty fresh herrings. They are packed with flavour and goodness; you'll find everyone feels better after eating them.

* Herrings are a rich source of protein.
* They contain protective Vitamin A.
* One fresh herring provides a day's needs of sunshine Vitamin D.
* Herrings contain calcium, phosphorus and iodine – all essential to health.
* Herrings give you lots of energy.
* – and KIPPERS, too, of course ! ! !

Give the youngsters herring – and see how they G-R-O-W

HERRING INDUSTRY BOARD

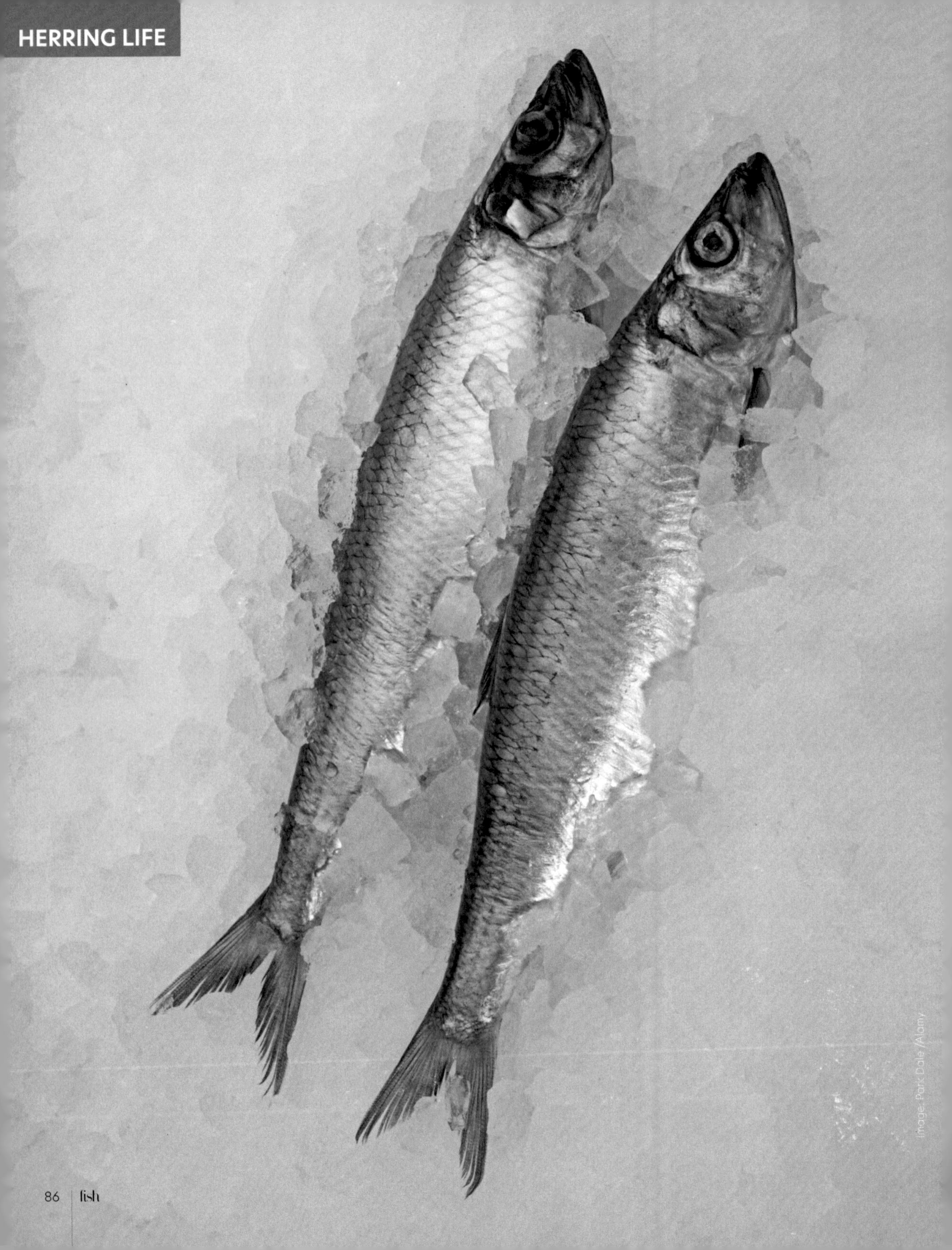

Image: Park Dale /Alamy

Silver darlings

It is perhaps the unsung hero of the sea. It is the ultimate prey fish, bounteous and nutritious. Yet it remains a great unknown, even amongst those who eat it regularly. It is the herring, and it is important.

Nathan Hill | Journalist

MY INTRODUCTION TO the herring was the standard for a child of a certain working-class heritage. A whole kipper, cleaved neatly from head to tail along its dorsal ridge, and pungent from the oak over which it had been smoked, became a dietary staple long before I had reached ten years of age.

In the mid-1980s, my hometown of Hastings was less a fishing port and more a tourist attraction, yet the fisherfolk and their vessels — a large inshore fleet that parked on shingle instead of in a harbour — laboured on. Much of my childhood protein came from their nets.

Butterflied and buttered, body akimbo on the plate, the fish was cooked as it should have been; grilled beneath real flames, the tail-tips scorched and charred. I recall bronzed flesh on a trellis of bones, flakes of meat coming away from translucent prongs as pliable and sharp as balsa. The skin, gunmetal and gold, clung on with a snail's footing of mucus. The flavours were more brutal than complex, the sensation enhanced by my underdeveloped palate, the salted butter the only defence from the acrid oils and scorched leather tones. Yet these were not unwelcome sensations. Eighties kids understood harsh tastes. We were the children raised on many cheaper cuts of meat, and after calves' liver and lambs' kidneys such a fish was an exorbitant treat. I loved the meal, forgave it for its gastric hostility, came to relish its appearance in the fridge.

Welcome to me, herring.

***

Image: Simon Maycock/Alamy

Above: *Herrings undergoing smoking into kippers.*

→

Herring. An established household name. A catch-all term that might describe many different species. If we use taxonomy to decide what really constitutes a herring, it could refer to one of two species: *Clupea harengus*, the Atlantic herring, or *Clupea pallasii*, the Pacific herring. We could be bold and call these the 'core' herrings. Be bold with me. These are the core herrings, and *Clupea harengus* is the most core of all.

Swing through the branches of the herring's taxonomic tree and we encounter close cousins; round herrings and thread herrings of *Jenkinsia*, *Etrumeus*, *Dayella* and *Gilchristella*, related to *Cluepa*, but far from core. Kin, maybe, but not kipper.

Then there are the apologists, incautious heretics who refer to any fish in the Clupeidae family as a herring, scooping up some 200 species of assorted menhadens, sardines and shads in one giant indiscriminatory trawl.

Beyond that, herrings by name but not taxonomy; hatchet herring, longfin herring, a freshwater salmonid optimistically named the Lake herring by mischief makers. Real herrings that aren't presented as such. Sild, a niche-taste fish sold in cans with oils or sauces, are simply juveniles from the *Clupea* genus. It is a bog of misattributed honorifics that needs a team of lexicographers to drain it.

***

Clupea harengus is, for us in the UK, the important herring, economically and ecologically, and it is stupendously abundant. Aside the deep-dwelling bristlemouths, herrings may be the most numerically significant fish to roam the oceans.

Stupendously abundant.

In your mind, picture a fictional block of water. Make it a mile long on each of its sides. A large shoal of Atlantic herring, distanced as they would be in the wild, and each occupying a personal space of some 50-100cm^2, would only just fit inside. If observations are to be believed, even this hypothetical cube might not be large enough for some of the shoals that visit the Nordic Sea, annually encroaching the fjords in a sexually driven pilgrimage.

Perhaps as many as four billion fish may form in a single gathering, and this species produces the greatest human harvest of any of the herrings. Of all the fish sold under the herring moniker, the Atlantic makes up at least half of the overall annual worldwide catch.

> To eat them is to make the UK more self-sufficient in the face of Brexit — currently we import some 70% of our seafood from overseas, while exporting 75% of what we catch

Yet it's a fish that many in the UK still take for granted. It ranks badly with native consumers, not coming close to the 'big four' choices of cod, tuna, salmon and haddock. The Marine Conservation Society waxes lyrical about this, making a sustainability pitch for the herring as an eco-friendly food. Herrings are found in local waters, the argument goes, and can be caught easily.

Image: Guy Harrop /Alamy

To eat them is to make the UK more self-sufficient in the face of Brexit. Currently we import some 70% of our seafood from overseas, while exporting 75% of what we catch — a whopping 93% in the case of herrings. Native herring consumption can help realign that imbalance, lowering food miles and carbon footprints into the bargain.

The importance of herrings to humans cannot be overstated. Wars have been fought, and towns and cities have been built around their collection and processing. Great Yarmouth owes its existence to them, originating as a herring fishing settlement shortly after the Norman conquest of 1066, the abundant food source eaten by both rich and poor, earning the fish the title of 'Silver darling'. Great Yarmouth retained its status as an important herring port until the late 1960s when the fish supplies temporarily dried up, and now hardly anyone fishes there; the boats that bob in its waters instead weighted down by gas, oil and consumer goods.

Globally, *Clupea harengus* has long presented an affordable source of protein. After ousting the Nazis in the 1940s, herring and potato represented the mainstay of the post-war Norwegian crisis diet, and many would have starved without it. They remain a staple there to this day, eaten salted and filleted, alongside boiled potatoes and pickled beets. The Dutch like them soused. The Germans like them canned, but also use rollmops to cure

Left: *93% of UK caught herrings are exported to Europe.*

Below: *Young Atlantic herring, Clupea harengus.*

Image: blickwinkel /Alamy

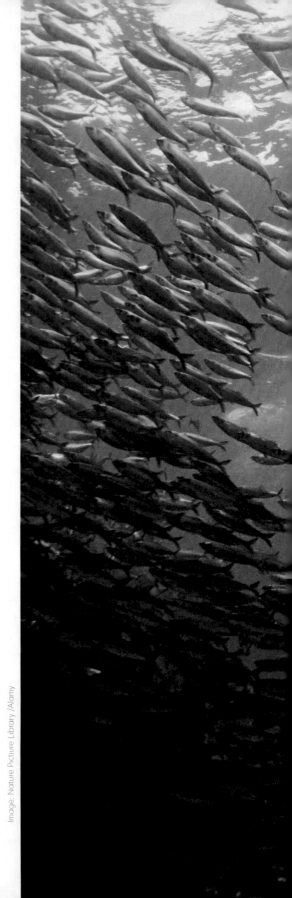

> ❝ Swimming inverted and flashing their white undersides, blowing bubbles and calling loudly to exploit the herrings' highly attuned hearing, the Orcas drive them close to the surface ❞

hangovers. The British still enjoy a breakfast kipper, while the Japanese have a soft spot for the soft spot, savouring the delicate briny roe. The Swedes even consume them on the cusp of rotting, in a dish called Surstromming. Sold in cans swollen to bursting point, some freighters refuse to touch them due to the risk of the cans exploding in transit. The fermented fish inside is ripened by anaerobic *Halanaerobium* bacteria, resulting in a food that's likened to sewage in both taste and texture. Numerous YouTube videos sit in homage to daring gastronomes who try, and fail, to eat it.

***

The demand for herring flesh extends from gourmets to gulls, and much in between. Many aquatic predators have evolved elaborate catching strategies to harvest the fish, like those of Humpback whales, which dive beneath a herring shoal and release a long stream of bubbles, swimming in a large circle to create a virtual lasso. Intimidated by the bubbles, the herrings are ushered into place in the middle of the ring, and it only remains for the whale to swim directly up through the aperture, mouth agape, to collect the stricken mass.

Nervous herrings form a bait ball as a defensive measure. Tightly packed in a writhing, reflective mass, predators struggle to pick out single fish for pursuit. But a bait ball is a short-lived and counterintuitive defence. For one, it is conspicuous, drawing attention to itself and acting as a beacon for even more predators. Worse still, with so many fish packed in so closely together, both swimming and breathing at elevated rates, the local oxygen supply is rapidly depleted. Any bait ball that lasts beyond ten minutes is a rarity.

Beyond Humpbacks, which might consume up to 2,000kg of fish per day, Orca whales have an equally complex relationship with herrings.

Right: An Orca whale stalks a herring shoal in Norwegian shallow waters.

Image: Nature Picture Library /Alamy

Orcas are sophisticated and specialised feeders, with different populations catering to different food groups. Around Norway, a site of considerable herring significance, the Orcas have evolved a 'carousel' method of capture.

Even when gathered as a tightly knit bait ball, the herrings are too fast and elusive for whales to pick off individually, so instead they choreograph. Swimming inverted and flashing their white undersides, blowing bubbles and calling loudly to exploit the herrings' highly attuned hearing, some Orcas drive them close to the surface. Others assist in compressing the terrified ball ever tighter, until a single whale swims close and strikes the edge of it with its tail, stunning several fish at a time.

Other predators aren't as refined. Gulls and gannets pluck from the surface or missile themselves into the water, hoping to spear a meal. Thresher sharks whip frenziedly through bait balls, concussing all and they touch with their lengthy,

lobed tails, before turning around to feast on the aftermath. Cod and halibut saunter up and use powerful oral suction to guzzle the hapless prey. More than this, several predators have learnt that easy pickings can be had from concussed fish leaping from, or spilling out of, a trawler's catch. Any fishing boat catching herrings will boast an impressive audience of followers.

And still the Atlantic herring prevails. For a while it almost didn't, population declines through the

> ‘ When they're not feeling frisky, herrings from separate populations may merge and swim together, but once the urges start to take hold they close ranks and migrate away to distinct offshore boudoirs ’

Left: *Gulls swamp a herring fishing vessel.*

1950s and 1960s ruining the Norwegian fishing towns that were reliant upon it. Around the UK, too, the herring was fished way beyond sustainable measures, with North Sea stocks collapsing through the 1970s, courtesy of no less than 14 different nations exploiting the struggling shoals. By January 1977, the British government was the first to declare a total ban on all herring catches, and by the end of June that year, other countries had all followed suit. The effects were profound. Between 1977 and 1980, the value of UK landed herrings dropped from close to £14 million to just £2 million, leading to widespread bankruptcy of ship owners, while a lack of supply saw the kipper plummet in popularity. By the early 80s, kipper processing was at an all-time low, and even after the fishing ban was lifted, kipper processing remained a shell of what it once was.

In the early 1990s, the UK witnessed was another decline, which led to an effective recovery plan in 1996. While this has generally been viewed as successful, as recently as January 2021 the marine conservation group Oceana reported that the stocks of Atlantic herring are being overexploited once more. By contrast, the International Council for the Exploration of the Sea, an intergovernmental science organisation that advises on fish stocks and quotas, sees less cause for concern, and their advice for 2021 includes an increase of herring catches in the northeast Atlantic, moving from an allowance of around 525,000 tonnes of fish in 2020 to some 650,000 tonnes for the current year. The International Union for Conservation of Nature, the global authority on the status of stocks in the wild, currently lists the Atlantic herring as 'least concern', but this listing is based on data for populations of the species worldwide, and remains so despite the fact that herring numbers in the North Sea have been at historically low levels for several years.

Stupendously abundant?

***

When Atlantic herrings come together to spawn, the resulting slurry of eggs and milt can be seen from orbit. The stains of reproduction spread for many miles, turning the surrounding seas milky white.

Around the UK there are three major herring populations, and each can be identified by its choice of timing and location for spawning. When they're not feeling frisky, herrings from separate populations may merge and swim together, but once the urges start to take hold they close ranks and migrate away to distinct offshore boudoirs. Between August and September, the Buchan or Shetland herrings meet up to spawn off of the coasts of Shetland. Somewhere through August to October, the Banks herrings meet to reproduce off of the English coast in the Central North Sea. Later than both, the Southern Bight of Downs herrings move further south to the English Channel, to breed in a window stretching from November to January.

While Atlantic herrings can spawn anywhere from two years of age, the majority adorn their purity rings and wait until they are three or four. To do so, they amass in one huge piscine orgy, millions of fish coming together at once. They are indiscriminate, the females producing ribbons of eggs, which the males fertilise from a few centimetres above them, releasing milt directly into the water. Egg numbers from females can vary pending age and population — a large female of 28cm from the Southern Bight population will release around 40,000 eggs at one time, while a similarly sized female from the Buchan population drops closer to 70,000. Immediately after this inelegant ceremony, the seabed may be inches thick with eggs.

Spawning takes place in shallow waters, no deeper than 40m. Herrings like to breed over sandy regions, often with seaweeds present, or across maerl beds — areas strewn with coral-like fragments. Pending the sea temperatures, hatching may take as little as six days when warm, and up to three weeks when cold. Upon hatching, the tiny fry — some 3-4mm long and a far cry from their adult forms — are reliant on a tiny sac of nutritious yolk, and that's all the help they get. Adult herrings have no time for outdated concepts like parental care, and simply assailing nature with sheer numbers of unloved young has served them well over the aeons.

Though abandoned, the young are at least not alone. The tiny herrings amass into a new shoal of juveniles, the spawning site becoming one huge nursery where they spend the next year — maybe two — growing and feasting on plankton, tiny sandeels, fish eggs and other organic flotsam. Only when substantially sized at 10cm or more do these nursery shoals migrate outwards into deeper water.

And that's it for the life cycle. Now shaped like their parents, the Silver darlings take up their own place in the wider ecology of the oceans, as one of Earth's most important forage fish; controllers of those animals smaller than them, vital protein for those larger. Of the tens of thousands of young created by each mother herring, only two need to make it back to the spawning grounds to continue the population. Until then, all that awaits is years of moving amongst the collective, avoiding the whales, sharks, gulls and nets that haunt every expanse of the open seas and perhaps, just perhaps, not ending up kippered. ∎

Opposite page: Buttered and grilled, a fine kipper.

Image: Panther media GmbH / Alamy

ATLANTIC HERRING / CLUPEA HARENGUS

Atlantic herrings can be surprisingly large fish reaching over 45cm fully grown, with a weight just over 1kg. Restrictions mean that around the UK, only fish larger than 20cm may be commercially harvested or kept by anglers. Lifespans are pretty well recorded, with an upper life expectancy of 15-16 years, though it is rare for one to reach this age.

They mainly eat plankton, swimming with mouths agape and using gill rakers to sift out tiny morsels as they ram feed through the water. Plankton isn't exclusive, and herrings are known to snatch small fish when presented with them.

Atlantic herrings have finely tuned hearing, something that can work against them — loud marine operations can cause considerable distress. They have evolved to use their hearing, combined with the period release of gas through the anus, to communicate with each other when in close proximity in the dark. This has led to international tensions in the past, most notably during the 1980s when the Swedish Navy mistook the sound of collective herring farts for Russian submarines intruding on its waters.

The fabled Red herring does not exist.

Iddisology

Form or function? Admire or eat? The Norwegian Canning Museum proves the both can exist in harmony.

Words: Graeme Rigby Images: Piers Crocker | The Norwegian Canning Museum

STAVANGER WAS capital of Norwegian sardine production. In 1879 the Stavanger Preserving Co. started it off, instantly winning first prize for their Smoked Norwegian sardines at Trondheim's fisheries exhibition. The city also gave birth to the collecting of sardine can labels: iddis — from iddikett, a street transmutation of etikett (label).

The last sardine factory in Stavanger closed in 1983, but by then it was already capital of Norwegian oil production. Reading the runes, the year before it had already opened the Norwegian Canning Museum, housing a collection of over 30,000 different iddis.

With paper labels predominating in Norway and the USA, collection was possible. Elsewhere in the world, a proclivity for printing directly on to the tin forces a choice between collection and consumption.

The iddis collection is a history in design and sales strategies, frequently beautiful, occasionally strange, always fascinating. Cigarette cards are about sets determined by narrative. Iddis just have constantly overlapping themes, each label determined by market idiosyncrasy and the endless mystery of mental association.

In 1920 Norway had 140 sardine canneries. The biggest player was Christian Bjelland & Co.'s King Oscar brand. In 2008 it shifted production to Poland and in 2014 was bought by Thai Union Group.

The Norwegian Canning Museum, on the other hand, which has been closed courtesy of the ongoing viral pandemic, reopens in Autumn 2021 with its glorious collection of tools, machines, memories and, of course, iddis. And it now has an entirely new printing museum next door, further opening up understandings of the wonderful world of labels.

Below: The Norwegian Canning Museum at Stavanger holds over 30,000 different sardine can labels.

Image: Lucas Vallecillos/Alamy

What is a fish pyramide? Artistic licence taken with a *stimenbildung* — a shoal's crowded excitement churning the surface in the constraint of a fjord? Or just artistic licence? Contemporary design sophistication runs through Norwegian sardine can labels. (1907)

Queen Victoria's face sold anything and inspired sardine marketing. King Oscar, Norway's pre-independence Swedish king, was actually more popular as Bjelland's sardine brand. Although hugely successful, growing markets demanded different brands, from King Saul to Amha, the son of Emperor Haile Selassie (Ras Tafari). (1954)

Vikings posing, trading or engaged in derring-do, proliferate on Norwegian sardine cans. Knud Bergslien's C19th painting portrays a 1206 civil war flight to safety with the two-year-old Haakon IV by members of the Birkebein or Birch-leg faction. (The Saga brand was first registered in 1914)

Vikings were, of course, Norsemen, who, frenched-up, became Normans, who became the aristocracy of Merrie England, singing across the seas to the sardine markets of the United States. (Tokstad-Burger Co. of New York established the Normanna brand in 1912)

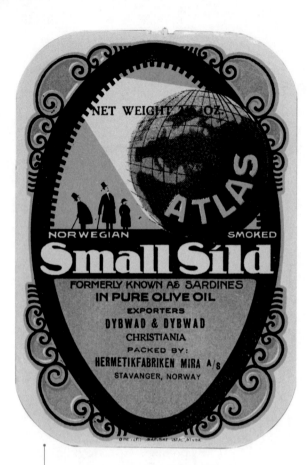

NET WEIGHT ... OZ.

ATLAS

NORWEGIAN SMOKED

Small Sild

FORMERLY KNOWN AS SARDINES
IN PURE OLIVE OIL
EXPORTERS
DYBWAD & DYBWAD
CHRISTIANIA
PACKED BY:
HERMETIKFABRIKEN MIRA A/S
STAVANGER, NORWAY

Terje Vigen (1862) is an Ibsen poem. To feed his starving family Terje runs an 1809 British naval blockade. With his bag containing barley (not fat herring) he's captured and his family all die. Years later he saves his own captor, as well as his captor's wife and child. (1931)

NETTOINNHOLD 105 GRAM
2 LAG 18/24 FISK

Terje Viken

PRIMA SOMMERFANGET
FET-SILD
I MARKOLOLJE

Norwegian sardines are small herrings (sild) or sprats (brisling). In the Great Sardine Litigation, finally settled in the English courts in 1915, the French successfully argued only European pilchards could be sardines, a ruling which still informs European labelling, but nobody else's. (c 1918)

Image: Colin Walton /Alamy

Swimming with dinosaurs

The bichirs are as ancient as they are odd looking. Existing over millions of years, they now face their greatest threat — change.

Joshua Pickett | The Bichir Handbook

Illustration: Dorian Noel

I T IS the late Cretaceous Period in what will eventually become North Africa. Drifting helplessly through the warm currents of an ancient river is a single small egg, spherical in shape and no larger than the thickness of a penny. Its parents were hardly attentive; they abandoned a multitude of eggs the moment they scattered them into the river's marginal plants. They didn't give much care as to how carefully they did so. There are dangerous animals in the margins, animals that come here for nothing more than hunting.

It's the ages-old evolutionary dilemma — why risk your own life protecting a few eggs, when you can just fertilise and disperse hundreds at once, abandoning them to the ravages of fate? Besides, the plants at this river's edge provide shelter. More, they carry a natural gift; an abundance of insect larvae to eat, the ideal larder for this couple's hungry, hatching progeny.

Above: *Polypterus bichir* and *Polypterus senegalus*, two modern bichir species.

➡

Not every egg has that luxury. Ours was flicked off by its father's clumsy tail and continues to drift, narrowly avoiding being consumed by roaming opportunists. As the river meanders, the egg is carried into the safety of a slow-moving bend, where it settles and sticks unnoticed to a fallen branch. Over the course of two weeks, the egg hatches and the marooned fry feeds on its yolk, all while still attached to the branch with a specialised pair of adhesive organs. The river's bend provides sanctity, and many larger fishes come here to escape strong currents. Yet even they are preyed upon by bigger, terrestrial piscivores. This young fish is going to have to be extraordinarily lucky to survive. These will be the only weeks of respite it will know, and its life will become ever more precarious. The world is a completely new and dangerous place.

The late Cretaceous, an era running from 100-66 million years ago, is an age of hungry goliaths, and the place our fish calls home is surrounded

Below:
Spinosaurus was a danger even to huge fish like Bawitius.

> Giant 3m long prehistoric fish like Bawitius stalk the waters, while semi-aquatic dinosaurs like Spinosaurus, growing to over 15m, skulk at the banks

by huge predators. Giant 3m long prehistoric fish like *Bawitius* stalk the waters, while semi-aquatic dinosaurs like *Spinosaurus*, growing to over 15m, patrol the banks.

Our fish is one of the earliest bichirs, a fish belonging to a primeval basal order known as the Polypteriformes. To our eyes now it would be almost unrecognisable from what we would consider a modern fish — its short, deep body has already adapted tough, inflexible, armoured scales, a row of closely set, sharp finlets along its dorsal (upper) edge, and spines in the pectoral (side) fins. At a glance, it might be mistaken for some small and chubby early crocodile. Few other fishes would want to eat it, even if they were large enough to do so.

The ancient remains of Polypteriformes have been found in both Africa and South America. The evidence suggests that they date back to a time before the continents split into the modern forms we know today. Genetic analyses place the ancestors of Polypteriformes back further still, back to the recesses of the Devonian era, some 360+ million years ago. Fossil evidence has only yielded a handful of specimens as far back as the late Cretaceous, but due to the huge differences between species of Polypteriformes in those remains we have found, this time period can be regarded as the peak of bichir diversity.

With all this in mind, we can start to paint a picture of the types of bichirs living in this time frame. The trend for early ray-finned (or Acinopterygii) fishes was for a short and deep body, quite unlike that which we see in modern bichirs. A problem arises because of huge gaps in the Polypteriform fossil

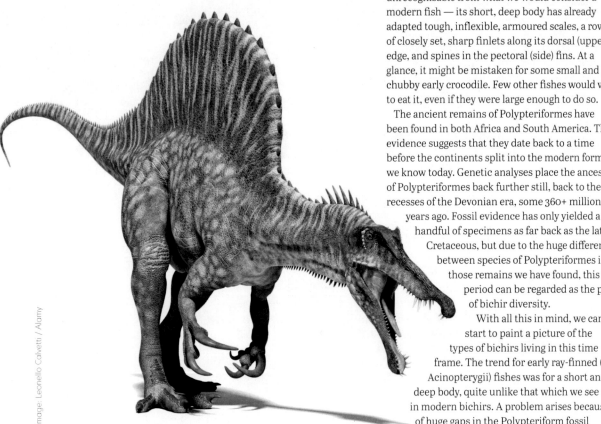

Image: Leonello Calvetti / Alamy

records, and any assertion about their evolutionary history trespasses into speculation. Still, from the information we can gather, most Cretaceous bichirs or older would have had shorter bodies than their notably lengthy descendants.

The elongated and distinctly snake-like bichirs we know today didn't adopt a serpentine shape across their family until after the Cretaceous, but probably had the Cretaceous to thank for it. What is clear is that adult Polypteriformes started to adapt for a benthic life on the substrate rather than free swimming in open water. This kept them away from the mainstay of the larger roaming predators of the time, and presented them ample opportunities to ambush prey rather than chase it.

66 million years ago, an asteroid collided with the Earth and wiped out most life in doing so. The bichirs were spared, though the landscape they inhabited was now permanently altered.

The flooding and isolated pools that formed in the asteroid's aftermath created many new ecological niches to explore. The early bichir survivors with the most elongate bodies were in the best position to traverse these new, shallow environments, allowing them to find spawning partners and pass on their genes. They became Darwinian success stories.

This pressure to evolve occurred again during a humid period from some 15,000 to 12,000 years ago, which led to the serpentine species of bichir we recognise today, along with another rise in bichir diversity. The most dramatic serpentine shape known to occur in Polypteriformes is of the Ropefish, *Erpetoichthys calabaricus*, an aquarium keeper's favourite that can grow to 45cm long while being no thicker than an AA battery. As their bodies grew longer, their pelvic fins receded until eventually disappearing altogether. If you're ever lucky enough to be one of the minority of people to

Above:
A modern Polypterus congicus with its serpentine form.

Illustration: Dorian Noel

Above & Top: Bawitius was a giant of its time, easily able to dwarf an adult human.

breed a Ropefish, closely check the embryo; you can see vestigial pelvic fins develop, only to then vanish during growth.

If you have ever seen or kept bichirs, you may notice that some have two branchy stalks behind their head — what we call external gills. These help the fish to extract oxygen from the water, in the same way that axolotls and other amphibians do. The gills are mostly seen in juveniles, but if the area they're living is unsafe, or if the water they're living in is low on oxygen, they may keep them throughout much of their early adulthood. Bichirs are bimodal breathers, able to utilise both atmospheric air from the surface and dissolved oxygen in the water through their external gills. Air breathing is facilitated by a primitive lung repurposed from the swim bladder; the internal chamber of air used by most other fish to maintain neutral buoyancy. Atmospheric air accounts for most of their oxygen intake, but in a

river or lake filled with larger predators, breaking cover and surfacing to breathe is dangerous. It's handy to have the backup of sufficient gills until you're large enough to avoid becoming lunch.

As well as being well adapted to avoid being eaten, bichirs are efficient predators themselves, and in some lakes and forest streams, they are the apex, feared by all. Being ill-equipped for high-speed or drawn-out pursuits, many have evolved to become ambush predators, sitting motionless on the substrate until prey swims by. Others creep, actively but slowly hunting through the shallow margins for resting fishes. What makes them so effective in either role is their powerful inertial suction, paired with needle-like teeth and rows upon rows of conical tooth patches that hold their prey in place. Inertial suction is created when the bichir rapidly opens its mouth; anything unfortunate enough to be in front of it is 'inhaled' at lightning speed, deep into that mouth of waiting dentition. For fishes too large to be swallowed whole, the struggle doesn't end there. In a manner akin to crocodiles, they can violently twirl to tear tissue from larger prey in motions called 'death rolling'. This is seen predominantly in smaller bichir species like *Polypterus retropinnis* that cannot swallow much of their natural prey whole.

Jaw protrusion within bichirs has evolved throughout history. The extant bichirs can be divided into two groups: upper jaw and lower jaw. The upper-jaw bichirs have an upper jaw equal

BAWITIUS / BAWITIUS BARTHELI

Bawitius bartheli, a long extinct early polypterid, lived through the Cretaceous Period and was found across what is now modern Egypt. At 300cm it was a gigantic fish, but living at a time of so many giants, it was still threatened by the many dinosaurs that roamed close to waterways. Uniquely, the fish had squared scales, as opposed to the (un)usual diamond shaped ganoid scales found on modern bichirs.

Image: Neil Hepworth/neilhepworth.com

Ropefish can reach 45cm while being no thicker than an AA battery.

Serenoichthys kemkemensis,
from the Cretaceous Period

Polypterus teugelsi,
a modern bichir shape

Polypterus endlicherii,
a lower jaw bichir

Polypterus palmas,
an upper jaw bichir

Illustrations: Dorian Noel

> The early bichir survivors with the most elongate bodies were in the best position to traverse these new, shallow environments, allowing them to find spawning partners and pass on their genes. They became Darwinian success stories.

to or longer than their lower jaw. These species are thought to share their jaw protrusion with the earliest bichirs. Then there are the lower-jaw bichirs, with lower jaws extending out further than the upper jaw. These species are relatively modern; the earliest lower-jaw bichir known to science was the now-extinct *Polypterus faraou*, dating back 11.6 million years. Lower-jaw bichirs have elongated, spoon-like head shapes, making their inertial suction stronger, as to feed on larger (or more distant) prey more effectively; another important adaptation contributing to their survival.

Some changes are occurring too fast for Polypteriformes and other fishes to adapt to. North Africa used to slowly transition between humid and dry periods, but 8,000-4,500 years ago, this transition became more rapid due to sudden overgrazing from farming. This led to reduced atmospheric moisture, resulting in what is now the Sahara Desert. Once their diversity hotspot, bichirs are now extinct throughout much of North Africa. Among the most northern species still existing today are a small, relict population of *Polypterus senegalus* surviving in a small oasis in the Sahara Desert. Even *Polypterus bichir* is thought to be extinct in Egypt, the country where bichirs were first discovered, though it still exists elsewhere. Man-made climate change has been in effect since we humans began to farm the lands we live on, and now it's accelerating. A fish can go from being widespread, to endangered, to extinct in quick succession. As for our collective sentiments towards them — fishes belong to a whole 'other world', out of sight and frequently out of mind. We give them very little protection.

If the bichirs continue to disappear across North Africa, not only has an unbroken lineage of Polypteriformes stretching back to the Devonian been lost forever, but we will also lose some of our own communities. Fishes caught for the aquarium trade can sell for over three hundred times the price they would in the food industry. Luckily for bichirs, they don't make great eating and take a long time to prepare, so entire villages may rely on aquarium exports as their main source of income. One species in particular, *Polypterus bichir*, is highly sought after in the aquarium trade, and just one individual is enough to keep the gears turning in a small community, so they only ever have to harvest a handful a year. As professional Cameroonian fisher Ngandu Jiku says: 'Collecting *Polypterus* for the aquarium trade has helped a lot of villages, because they can feed from the money when it sells. It has become one of the easiest ways to feed our community, and also pays for children to go to school. This fish has produced many jobs for us.'

It's almost painfully obvious, but to support bichir populations, one of the best things we can do is take steps to reduce our collective carbon footprints. That might be something as negligible as sending one less email a day or riding a bike to work. An extinction of any fish species is a tragedy told over a thousandfold, and we've potentially lost hundreds with at least a thousand currently classed as critically endangered. The lineages left behind by that drifting egg, the egg that survived the dinosaurs, the egg that survived predation from other fishes and even survived major extinction events, are all relatively unchanged.

It would be disturbing for these truly ancient fishes to vanish forever because of our actions. ∎

BICHIRS / POLYPTERIDAE

Polypterids are old and archaic looking fish, considered a sister group to all other existing bony fishes. Amongst their unique features are the broad and fleshy pectoral fins, giving them a look similar to equally ancient fishes like Coelacanths. Even their scales are distinctly un-fishy, with a diamond shape that only adds to their snake-like appearance.

They tend to inhabit sluggish rivers or swampy, marshy habitats such as estuaries and floodplains, and here they spend their time feeding on insects, crustaceans, fish and even small mammals. Being primarily nocturnal predators, their eyesight is relatively poor, but this is made up for by an extremely powerful sense of smell.

Despite their predatory nature, bichirs are hugely popular in the aquarium industry as 'oddballs' — quirky curiosities that can be kept in a domestic setting. Species can range from relatively small at some 30cm or so, up to heavyset brutes of around 1m.

full bladders

Plenty of fish graze on plants, but can the tables be turned?
Are there plants that make their living from eating fish flesh?

Ian Hodgson | Horticultural Author

CAN CARNIVOROUS plants that thrive in lakes and rivers eat fish? It may seem an outlandish, but there is anecdotal evidence to extrapolate the idea. On land there are pitcher plants, *Nepenthes*, in the Philippines large enough make a meal of an unfortunate rodent. Perhaps it follows that, although much smaller in size, the submerged spring traps of a Bladderwort, *Utricularia* sp., could feast on fry or even small fish. This piscivory is mentioned in some descriptions of *Utricularia vulgaris*, one of four bladderwort species that inhabit the ponds and ditches of Great Britain, and *U. gibba*, a plant well-known to aquarium and pond keepers. But is it true?

Ever since naturalist Charles Darwin published his ground-breaking study 'Insectivorous Plants' in July 1875, mankind has been fascinated by what are more popularly and luridly termed 'carnivorous plants'. Outlandish organisms like the Venus flytrap, Sundew, Pitcher plant and Bladderwort are hungry for animal flesh, and evolved from a common ancestor somewhere between 8 and 72 million years ago. Today we know that 12 different plant families, spanning 20 genera and 583 species, developed an astonishing rage of lures, traps and stomachs to escape competition from more agile, profligate plant life by inhabiting austere, nutrient-poor habitats both on land and in water.

The lack of essential nutrients needed to sustain life, such as nitrogen, placed evolutionary pressures on ancestral plant forms to overcome the debilitating challenges, and they did so by supplementing their nutrition through insidiously digesting the corpses of hapless, captured wildlife.

Utricularia, the most recently evolved and numerically largest carnivorous plant group, has around 240 described species, with more being found in remote parts of the world all the time. Although possessing one of the smallest genomes of any flowering plant, bladderworts possess the remarkable ability to evolve quickly to exploit new habitats, hence the wide number of species in existence on every continent except Antarctica. *Utricularia gibba* has a vast geographic range and occurs naturally in the United States, Canada, Central and South America, Spain, Israel, most of Africa, most of Asia including China and Japan, Australia and the North Island of New Zealand. Around 84% of bladderworts are terrestrial, living on soil, rocks and even on trees. The other 16% are aquatic, floating freely in acidic or peaty water, generally in lowland lakes, ponds, slow-flowing streams and ditches.

Utricularia all produce a slender network of stems, with rudimentary leaves capturing small organisms by means of bladder-like suction traps, recognised as one of the most sophisticated structures in the plant kingdom. The tiny traps range from 0.2mm to 1.2cm and when their sensitive trigger hairs are activated there is rapid release of elastic instability, among the fastest in the plant world. Water is pumped out ionically through the thin bladder walls to create negative internal pressure to the water outside. When the trapdoor is triggered both prey and surrounding water are sucked into the bladder in a process taking just ten to fifteen milliseconds. An eye-blink takes 300 milliseconds, or a third of a second. Once the bladder is full the door closes again and a digestive enzyme is released to dissolve the victim — pending the size of the prey it takes from a few hours to a few days to consume each catch.

Although traps are usually only large enough for water fleas or nematodes, *Utricularia* species with larger traps such as *U. vulgaris* and *U. gibba* are sometimes described as taking larger prey such as fish fry and tadpoles. Alas, this appears to be a fiction. Nobody seems to have physically recorded this happening, even though some observers have spent considerable time trying to obtain a sighting, but perhaps there is a yet to be discovered species in a pond somewhere that routinely does.

Sadly, it is humankind that is currently giving these carnivorous plants indigestion. Recent research from Japan has shown that microplastic particles sucked into *Utricularia vulgaris* are toxic, stunting growth and affecting the functionality of traps. That makes *Utricularia* a potentially useful bio-indicator of microplastic pollution in freshwater ecosystems, which really is food for thought. ∎

Above: *Bladderwort traps are extremely sophisticated.*

Below: *Utricularia flowers distract from the plant's predatory nature.*

Marlin
at a glance

A marlin is a marlin, is a marlin, right? Not at all. There are several species of these dashing predators. Here are some of them.

Words: Nathan Hill, Illustrations: Madhusudhan Gundappa

mARLINS. HANDSOME, high-velocity apex predators. The swashbucklers of the sea, armed and dangerous, and wielding their rapiers menacingly in their pursuit of prey. Marlins belong to a predatory group of fish known more broadly as the billfish, and billfish are easy to spot. Just as whiskers make a catfish, so a prominent bill makes a billfish.

Unlike the bills of the famous Swordfish, *Xiphias gladius*, which are long and bladed, those of marlins are shortened and spear-like, but can still be used to devastating effect. Plunged into a writhing mass of sardines, a quick cut and thrust can stun, cleave and kill indiscriminately. Open the belly of any marlin, and amongst its meals you'll find fish gashed and split in two.

What marlins don't tend to do is impale, beyond the accidental. Only a few underwater stabbings appear intentional — a handful of Mako and Great white sharks have been found bayonetted, with a bill run through them. Mistakes are made, though. Small, free-swimming pelagic fish have a tendency to congregate around floating objects, whether those objects are drifting clumps of *Sargassum* seaweed or a fisherman's boat at rest. To a hungry marlin, it makes no difference. The gathering of fish presents an opportunity for lunch, and the marlin will lunge at it with its sharp rostrum, with no regard for any hapless fisherman minding his business above. Human stabbings are rare, but they happen; usually a recreational fisherman impaled on his marlin at the closing stages of a catch, as the desperate fish leaps from the water and into the boat.

To humans, marlins are as prized for sport as they are for food. These fish are both large and powerful. One species may reach speeds of close to 70mph in short bursts, the fastest of any fish alive, while the considerable strength and endurance of others makes them a formidable angler's conquest. Sport fishermen routinely operate tag and release programs on any billfish they catch, working in tandem with conservationists and helping to gather data that would be otherwise unobtainable.

Opposite page: A Striped marlin, Kajikia audax, menaces a ball of bait fish.

Black Marlin / *Istiompax indica*

At a recorded length of 4.65m and a potential weight of 750kg, the Black marlin can rightly claim to be one of the largest bony fish on the planet. Throughout their lives, they migrate vast distances; one fish tagged in California later turned up over 6,500 miles away in New Zealand. Some erroneous reports suggest the Black marlin is the fastest of all the billfish, with a supposed top end of 80mph, though this is disputed.

White marlin / *Kajikia albida*

If the White marlin ever stops swimming, it will die. The fish is a ram ventilator, pushing water across its gills as it moves. Though long — adults will reach a potential 2.8m — the fish is lean, and the largest ever on record only weighed 82kg. Sport fishing for this species is contentious. Even with a catch and release approach, the White marlin may become so exhausted during its time thrashing about that when eventually set free it does not recover. Studies suggest that around a third of White marlin released by fishermen fail to recover their buoyancy.

Mediterranean spearfish / *Tetrapturus belone*
Perhaps the palates of Southern Europe are finicky, but the Mediterranean spearfish is often given an easy ride by those who release it upon catching — the flesh isn't revered by locals already spoiled with rich seafood choices — why waste time with a mediocre meal when you have Bluefin tuna and Swordfish available in the same waters? While other billfish tend to migrate and cover vast distances over their lives, this species has found its niche throughout the Mediterranean, and it stays there for its whole five-year life.

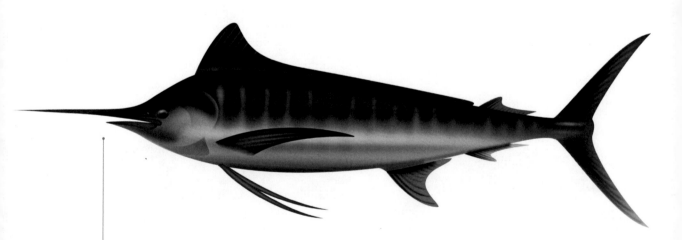

Indo-Pacific blue marlin / *Makaira mazara*
A challenging fish for the taxonomists, the Indo-Pacific blue marlin may be an identical species to the Atlantic blue marlin, *Makaria nigricans*. Going by the genetic data, at least, both fish are one and the same. The Indo-Pacific is the hot-house flower of the marlin crowd, being the least likely to stray away from equatorial waters. It's also one of the least likely to venture anywhere close to land, preferring the open expanse of the sea. Reaching 5m fully grown, it is the longest of any marlin.

→

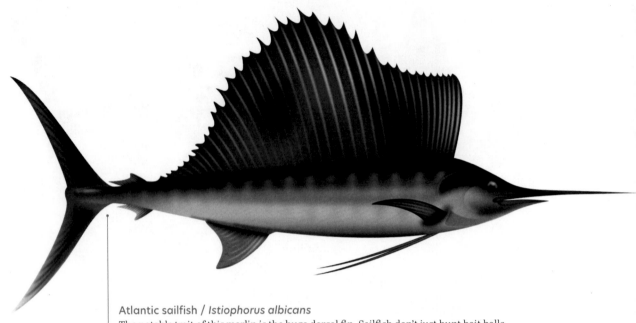

Atlantic sailfish / *Istiophorus albicans*

The notable trait of this marlin is the huge dorsal fin. Sailfish don't just hunt bait balls of fish, they sculpt them, using their magnificent fins to herd their prey together before striking. Rarely, they will come together in groups to feed, which introduces the risk of accidentally spearing each other. In order to avoid this, they communicate in colours, expressing their intentions to those around them by shifting from blue, to striped, then to black as they make their feeding runs. The high density of blood vessels in the sail suggest that it may also act as a biological solar panel, raised when the fish is just below the water's surface to absorb heat during the day.

Longbill spearfish / *Tetrapturus pfluegeri*

Something of an enigma in the billfish world, little information exists about the Longbill — it wasn't even recognised as a species until as late as 1963, while the first billfish was described over 170 years earlier. What data we have suggest a short lived and small fish, reaching a maximum of 2.5m and a lifespan of perhaps five years. Despite the moniker, the bill length is pretty unremarkable when compared to other marlins.

Shortbill spearfish / *Tetrapturus angustirostris*
A fish that lives up to its name, the diminutive Shortbill has the least impressive rostral ornament of any marlin. While it only has limited potential for slashing at passing shoals, the pointed snout aids with hydrodynamics, helping the fish to swim more efficiently. Barely reaching some 2m fully grown and with a weight of around 50kg at most, few commercial fisheries bother with it. Where it is caught, it often ends up as an ingredient in fishcakes, sushi or sausages.

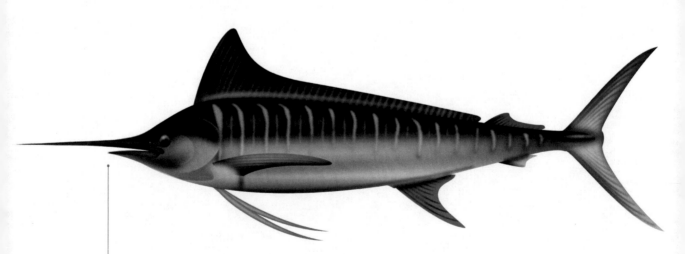

Striped marlin / *Kajikia audax*
The Striped marlin is amongst the most prized of the billfish for the flavour of its flesh, usually destined for a Japanese audience who prize it as sushi and sashimi. In some parts of the world, marlin flesh is prohibited from being sold as food, due to its high content of mercury. As mercury is bioaccumulative, old and large fish tend to build up more of it than smaller, short-lived species. With a potential lifespan of some twenty years for females, the Striped marlin has plenty of time to reach toxic levels. ■

Lost
at
sea

Nursery and warzone, packed with sustenance
yet ruthlessly cruel — countless fish join, become,
exploit, and leave the world of plankton every day.
They're just so small that we barely notice it.

Tim Smith | Ichthyologist

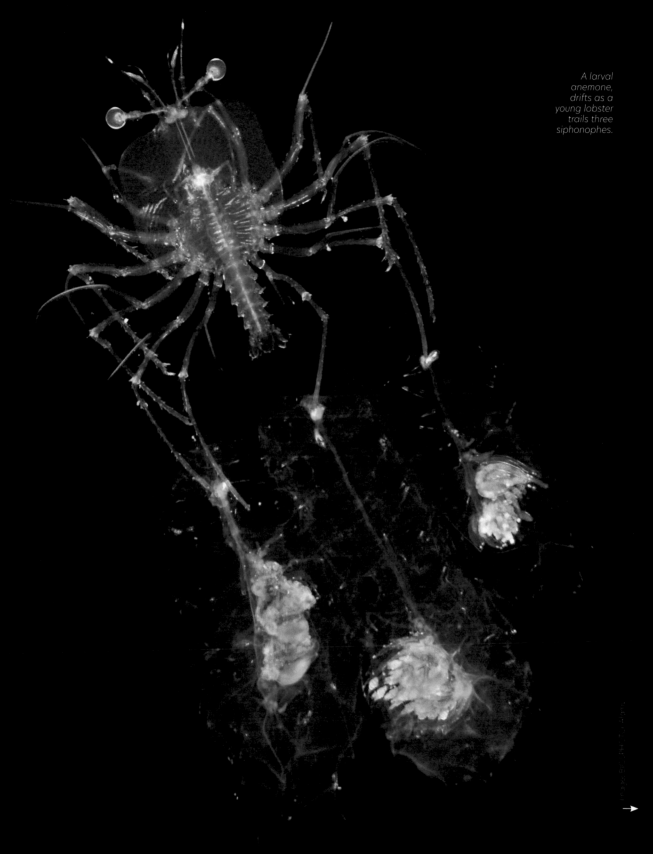

A larval
anemone,
drifts as a
young lobster
trails three
siphonophes.

Image: Paulo Oliviera, Alamy

THE ENORMITY of the ocean ecosystem can distract us from the fundamental machinery of its operations. Due to their size, plankton give an illusion of absence in a role that underpins the very functioning of the ocean at large. Contributing about a fifth of the total biomass in the oceans and outnumbering larger lifeforms by orders of magnitude, plankton play a part in the life cycles of virtually all marine life, often more directly than not.

Fish are intricately woven into the planktonic picture in contribution, participation, and predation. Fish eggs and larvae representing thousands of species are cast into the ocean throughout the year, contributing significant biomass to the planktosphere. Once there, planktonic larvae play an important role as both predators and prey to fellow plankton. Finally, plankton are a critical food source for innumerable marine species, from the larvae of tiny blennies to gargantuan adult whale sharks.

Looking so drastically different from their adult appearance, many planktonic larvae were long assigned to their own species, until such a time as scientists were able to directly observe the growth

Image: BIOSPHOTO, Alamy

of these creatures into a more familiar form. More recently, DNA analyses can quickly help assign bizarre larval forms to the right species.

Any planktonic larval form is necessarily different to its eventual adult manifestation. It's not just a matter of scaling — the planktosphere is an alien world unto itself. Forget regular swimming, for example. At plankton's diminutive size, the sheer viscosity of water means that active swimming is largely futile, and energy is saved for short bursts towards prey, or away from a would-be predator. All other travelling is left to the will of the current.

Above: Plankton is a primary food source for filter feeders like anchovies.

Below: A larval Swordfish will eventually be a giant, but for now it is amongst the smallest of creatures.

It's a life and death race for mass in the liquid throng and there is urgency to growing up.

If swimming differs so significantly, so too does bodily form, and a larval fish's body will change remarkably several times over before it resembles anything we might readily recognise. These changes reflect both the dynamic relationship the small animal has to its physical environment, as well as pressures and food sources it encounters as it grows.

When a part of the planktonic world, young fish are known as ichthyoplankton. Here they are represented by their eggs and larvae, and only leave once they've developed into juvenile forms that are no longer reliant on currents to usher them around. It may sound helpless to rely on water flow for travel, but being a tiny surfer confers certain advantages.

Riding with the current is a great means for dispersal, especially when swimming is not an option, both as a physical challenge as well as relative distance to be covered. This helps the young settle in new, suitable environments, as well as catching a ride with all manner of other helpless plankters that will serve as food. And by being scattered far and wide, you're a lot less likely to find yourself ending up alongside and spawning with one of your own siblings — a problem for creatures that never travel. In exploiting this easy means of distribution, parents don't need to invest a lot of energy into a few young, as mammals do with their demanding offspring,

Image: BIOSPHOTO, Alamy

but rather can hedge their bets with thousands — sometimes even millions — of eggs that are cast out into the blue void.

On the flip side, life as plankton comes with inherent dangers. Fish eggs and larvae would seem to function more as a food source than anything else. Of the trillions of eggs produced, nearly all of them — 99% by some estimates — surrender their resources back to nature through predation or other mortality. This seems like a massive loss, but playing the numbers game, still leaves billions of larvae to push through to juvenility and hopefully beyond.

Most species spawn at particular times of year in order to match up their young hatching with peak planktonic blooms. The timing here is critical — if hatching occurs outside of this abundance, most if not all of the fry will starve. As eggs, and for some time as newly hatched larvae, planktonic fishes remain adrift, offering little interaction with the surrounding biosphere except as a food source. Even once hatched, the young may still depend on an attached, life-sustaining yolk sac, feeding on the nutrients of their embryo to survive.

During this time, further development takes place. Quite importantly, the fish gain a mouth. This happens not long before they switch over to feeding on other organisms, but they are still remarkably inefficient feeders. A tiny gape, unspecialised digestive tract, and a paucity of hunting capabilities do little to help hunting successes.

Only once additional development takes place do they become true little predators. Capable senses with which to detect prey, a bigger mouth, a digestive tract that can better utilise resources, and musculature that propels them toward a desired food item are great tools to have, but the developing young are still a long way off from adulthood. As time goes by, learned behaviours will add to their hunting repertoire and prey capture successes will mount.

Growth happens at a mind-boggling rate among larval fishes, with the most significant increases in mass and size by as many as three orders of magnitude during this time. The trick is to live in a suspended medium of food, and that is precisely what planktonic larvae do. Such ready access to food sources, often of great variety, ensures that the developing young can feed almost continuously. Variety is great for health, but is critical for growth. →

This is not just for putting on size, but for locating new prey items that meet the demands of a now larger animal. These youngsters are growing at such a rate that the minuscule prey items previously sought might not be worth the effort anymore. Progressively larger items can be found either by changing what animals they might be eating, or by taking advantage of the fact that many other species within the planktosphere are growing up, too.

It's a life and death race for mass in the liquid throng and there is some urgency to growing up. Smaller fishes are more vulnerable to predation and in many cases it is critical to 'escape' certain size classes that are ripe for the picking in the eyes of would-be predators. Unfortunately, not all plankton are viable food choices, for all the quantity and variety that abounds. Plankton is chiefly made up of five trophic ingredients: phytoplankton, zooplankton, mycoplankton, bacterioplankton and virioplankton. Zooplankton is the animal component, the tiny crab larvae, coral polyps in waiting, and fish, while phytoplankton is the vegetable side of the equation, in the form of microscopic algae. It is the phytoplankton that is praised for producing so much oxygen, and it's estimated that up to 80% of Earth's oxygen originates with these floating plant cells. The remaining three plankton types consist of fungi, bacteria and viruses.

Below: A larval Lionfish, already showing its magnificent fins.

Opposite page: An isopod hitches a ride on a larval moray eel.

Despite remarkable abundance and suitable size classes, many species of phytoplankton make poor food sources for growing marine larvae. This is in part explained by their notably low nitrogen content, largely expressed as proteins, which is a critical requirement for any rapidly growing animal. The underdeveloped guts of very young larvae also lack the adaptations that are required to efficiently process algae, making it an empty resource to utilise, at least initially.

Other planktonic species have made incredible efforts to prevent being eaten, and fishes are no exception. Tiny animals have equally tiny mouths, and so it is common among many forms of plankton to have extravagant spines and structures that make capture and swallowing quite difficult. These structures will disappear before adulthood, but in the meantime they contribute to the many bizarre forms we see among fish larvae.

How long a fish remains in larval form, and sometimes by extension a planktonic member, varies from species to species. Some fish might only spend a few weeks among their fellow plankters, while eels are examples of fish that may spend many months in this state. In order for a larva to graduate into a juvenile, it needs to metamorphose. This is more than a simple cosmetic change, although appearances can shift drastically at this stage. The process of metamorphosis is an energy-demanding endeavour and includes the acquisition of adult features and the loss of larval ones; this shift equips the fish to move freely within its environment and utilise new food and environmental resources. At this point, the fish is now a juvenile and by most definitions, loosely resembles the adult form. Critically, to leave the plankton landscape, one must be able to locomote under one's own steam.

Once this stage has passed, ties to the planktonic world may not yet be severed. Many fishes will still rely on planktonic food sources throughout their juvenile years; the adults of some species never give it up. Even outside of planktivory, these same animals eventually give back to the world in which they grew up: casting their eggs into the currents to become a part of planktonic realm, contributing to a dynamic which they were once so intimately involved in years before, and beginning the life cycle anew. ∎

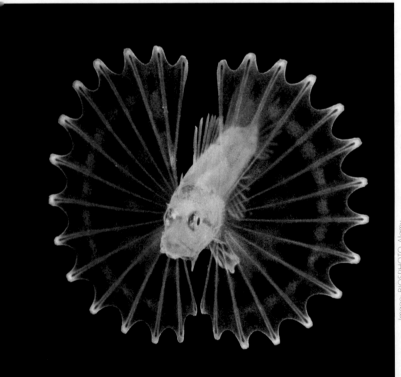

Image: BIOSPHOTO, Alamy

Plankton relationships graded by size

SIZE	EXAMPLES	RELATION TO ICHTHYOPLANKTON
Picoplankton 0.2 to 2μm	Bacteria and other simple organisms	An important energy source for the prey items of small fish larvae
Nanoplankton 2 to 20μm	The smallest examples of phytoplankton	These represent the smallest foods available to larval fishes, and are important to their prey items
Microplankton 20 to 200μm	Most phytoplankton, alongside small animal life and the larval forms of crustaceans	Includes some of the most important food sources for newly hatched marine larvae
Mesoplankton 0.2 to 20mm	Many smaller crustaceans alongside the young of other pelagic species. Many newly hatched larval fish would fall into this category.	Important for progressively larger larvae and juveniles; some may act as predators of larval fish.
Macroplankton 2 to 20cm	Larger pelagic species, often with adult representatives including many jellies, krill, and other crustaceans. Large larvae and metamorphosed juveniles fall into this category.	Many animals in this category are important predators of smaller size classes of plankton, including fish eggs and larvae.

grinning

Nathan Hill

TONY AND Karen are the last through the door, marking just shy of eighty customers. I offer them wine, but Tony protests. He's driving home after this gig, so I insist on a softer option. 'Company policy, everyone's having a drink tonight,' I say, punctuating myself with a smile. 'We've spent good money on tonight's bash, everyone needs to have fun.'

Karen snatches the alcohol from me, her tubby fingers reaching out like some hungry baby for the Chateaux-le-crap in plastic cups. Karen isn't driving. Karen is happy to fill up on my free wine, with no regard for flavour or lack thereof. Karen's whole existence is low resolution and tonight is a high point for her.

Tony breeds colourful guppies in tanks in his garage, glass boxes scaffolded on some jerry-built rack. That's why he's here tonight, to score a discount on my newly arrived Malaysian fish, some of the nicest stock from the best breeders we have. I helped him with the gear for his set up, offered him ten percent off if he bought a job lot of hardware from me. Every time he's in he shows me pictures of his latest, worthless hybrids on an iPhone with a cracked screen.

A couple of months back Tony posted in a local Facebook group about us. 'Overpriced,' he wrote. 'Fish section is shit and guy who runs it a proper no it all.' He couldn't even spell 'know' right.

As I'm reaching around for his drink, I notice the emblem on my polo shirt, the shirt provided by Companionz Petz. In stitching made from a thousand, cross threaded lines, the single word 'manager' tells customers and staff alike that I am in charge.

***

Five weeks ago the employee we called Grinner killed himself in the car park. Grinner was intelligent, but not on-paper intelligent. He hadn't formally studied aquatics the way I had, never had an accountant father to fund him through four years of university on the Scottish coastline, counting blennies in freezing rockpools, slicing thumbs on rocks sheeted in barnacles.

'What was it like in Peru?' he'd ask. He'd been jealous of my background, jealous that I'd travelled abroad to see the very fish that he so adored. I'd share stories of shoals that danced around my toes, picking at dead flesh. Tiny catfish with serrated fins that ate the gills of other fish and tried to get down the end of your penis if you pissed in the water. He'd soak it up. Any money he'd earned was thrown straight back in the tills. More tanks, more fish, more immersion, more hobby. I had to record every single employee purchase in a special discount book that head office insisted on and never read; hand written receipts in triplicate and a faded carbon print given to the staff member. Somehow it always felt like a diabolical contract, like the company owned a little bit more of you with each purchase.

Grinner's death got a mention in some dingy local newspaper. He was on page four, a small box elbowed out by some feature on a Z-list celebrity coming to town to do panto. Chris Edwin Grindle. Suicide. So sad. Goodbye.

Most of the staff at my branch were shop floor useless. They'd drop things, give customers the wrong change, dole out bad advice. Take Jobe, the head of dry goods purchasing. His real name was Joe

and he was overweight. We handed out nicknames more often than pay rises at Companionz Petz. Jobe had called me over one day when he was unpacking some boxes. He'd looked pleased with himself, like the slowest kid in class finally working out algebra, wanting to show something wonderful off to the world. He'd bought up a load of flea killer, in tiny ampules that you emptied onto a dog's neck. The packets were more skull and crossbones than product name, and there were several large boxes packed with them, some clearance offer he'd secured with one of the seedier sales reps. He'd handed me the invoice and told me to look. Three hundred packs at under a pound each. Enough to clear the parasites from a whole town.

'I'm retailing them for the same as the others,' he'd told me. 'Nine ninety-nine. Have you any idea what the profit margin is on that?'

Just a few days later the government enacted some legislation that had been in the pipeline for years, something anyone would know if they'd bothered to do a Google search on it. It turned out this stuff was putting people into hospital, had damn near killed a kid in London, so they banned it. Jobe quietly dragged it off the shelf, stuck the whole lot in the store room and never mentioned it again.

We'd sold three packets.

Grinner had been in it for the animals. He'd come in on his days off just to check on them. He'd had favourites. I'd put him in charge of the fish section, his passion and gift. He'd never gotten a polo shirt with manager written on it, but he did get a special key that allowed him behind the livestock systems; an insignificant prestige. Inside a month of him starting, that section outshone the rest of the store, a plastic diamond in a fool's gold mine.

'Do you, uh... do you ever feel bad about selling these things?' he'd once asked. From that moment, I was hooked on him. Companionz Petz policy was that we couldn't refuse a sale. Some jobsworth at head office had even wangled it into our contracts. Giving advice was the only weapon available at the frontline in our fight for animal welfare.

Grinner's relationship with customers had been reciprocal, and they'd hated each other. He used to hand me the phone when he got a complaint in, holding it down and cupping the mouthpiece before bringing me the latest terrible news from the world of aquatic sales. Complaints came in least daily and it would always fall to me, the manager, to manage them.

'The woman from yesterday, she's on line two. She wants a refund. All those tetras that I told her not to buy got eaten. She's saying her catfish had the lot.'

I'd shake my head, quip a quiet 'Fuck's sake' or something and take the handset. 'Why of course,' I'd say, 'we'll obviously replace the lot for you, maybe something more suitable this time. Yes, yes, come and see myself, I'll tend to it personally.' Grinner would just look at me in a way that damned me right to my soul.

He'd killed himself on a Saturday, our busiest day. He'd looked drained all morning, barely animated by his daily staples of caffeine and Marlboro, and spent any free time going over to the guppy tanks and staring, just watching them, then he'd chuckle and shake his head at some private comical insight. Like Tony, he'd had a thing for them, used to breed his own lines, would show them at any clubs he could afford to travel to. He'd had an Instagram page set up for them, but nobody really followed it.

The last customers he'd ever served were a thirty-something couple, stocky and dumb looking; I'd clocked them as potential shoplifters. The man had some bullshit inked up the side of his neck, while his wife stood trying not to drool over herself. They'd not listened to a word Grinner said, swatting away advice like midges getting up their noses.

'I'll take the risk,' tattoo-neck kept saying. Grinner had given them what they wanted, and I'd looked at him while he was taking their money. I'd never seen him so pale.

That was about half-three. After they'd left, he'd gone out like always, a ten-minute afternoon break and smoke in his car. Whether he'd lit up I don't know, but while there he'd picked up the rifle he'd borrowed from his rabbit-hunting brother, slipped the dangerous end into his mouth, and put a single round into his skull. I heard later that there had been no exit wound. The bullet had gone in and just pinged around inside, a lead pinball bouncing around his brain, flesh to mush, Grinner to cadaver.

We'd shut the store the next day, stuck up a generic 'situations beyond our control' note on the door. Our Facebook account was wild, a little 'Sorry to hear about your incident (but give me details, Lord give me the graphic DETAILS)' mixed in with plenty of 'Bang out of order, desperately needed dog food, taking my custom elsewhere'. You couldn't visit any of the local pet groups without seeing a post about

it. 'I knew he wasn't right, probably go bust now, was shit there anyway'.

Two days later, big bosses I'd never even seen before suddenly appeared in my office, scratching through my paperwork like I was a newsagent. They took me out for food and a talk, wined and dined by the cream of Companionz Petz' head office, most of whom didn't know my name.

'We're worried,' one had said. 'The way events like this are handled can have a real effect on turnover.'

I'd switched off over the next hour while they'd talked, me the nodding audience as they fixed everything. I'd watched as they'd vomited business jargon at each other, prompting me for an occasional confirmation of some rhetorical question.

'So, it's agreed,' another had eventually said. 'A conceptual reset starting with an open night. We'll authorise a case or two of wine and some nibbles. You can organise the catering. Get the punters in and engage them as community. Get them onside with the rebrand to follow. Do it right and they'll become our unwitting ambassadors.' Not a single one of them had asked how I was coping.

Three days after that meeting, tattoo-neck and drooling woman had returned to complain. Everything they'd bought was dead. They'd wanted replacements, plus more for the inconvenience. Their kid had been upset, had cried its eyes out when all the fish died. I'd gone through some details of the transaction with them. Apparently, Grinner had said that everything would be fine. Apparently, Grinner should be the one paying for their fish. Apparently, Grinner had been a rude twat. I'd given them replacements, in line with company policy, along with a credit note to spend whenever they liked. I'd smiled the whole time and trilled my diplomat's voice. I'd made them feel as though they'd been the victims of some terrible injustice, but that I, the manager, had fixed everything. Afterwards, I'd gone to the store room and bawled my eyes out, slumped behind the boxes of Jobe's unsellable flea killer.

Jobe arranged the catering for the open night. He had a cousin who did food for weddings, and it had been clear from the offset that Jobe was taking the piss with the figures. He'd wave sheets under my nose, pointing at sums and reassuring me of

smiling my professional smile to all along the way, reaching out to touch people with one hand, a polite gesture of acknowledgement, letting them know that each and every one of them is special to me. Their patronage means a lot to us at Companionz Petz.

I pass Geoff, grinning at me from beside a big reef aquarium he's been eyeing up since we first got it in. Geoff recently posted in the Fishkeepers North South East and West group on Facebook that we're the worst shop he knows, but that 'the girl on the rabbit section has a great ass lol'. His comment brought him almost ninety reactions, hearts and laughing faces, scowls, hugs and blue thumbs in a rebus of emojis.

Mike, currently fawning over tortoises he can't afford, likes to share the same meme every couple of weeks on our store's online forum, images of Robert Downey Jr. rolling his eyes alongside the caption 'When you know more than the pet shop staff'. When not exercising his considerable intellect, Mike works in a factory putting pickles in jars for minimum wage, same as he's done for fifteen years.

And Gary, who could miss Gary? Gary's wife left him when he tore out half his own kitchen to build an indoor pond, lined with porcelain tiles and kept clean by a repurposed koi filter. I saw it in the flesh once, when I went to drop off a replacement pump part for him. The whole house reeked of urine and nitrogen. Gary's contribution to the world of collective online wit came under a post somewhere that mentioned Grinner's death. 'Guess he couldn't handle his shots,' he wrote. He even liked his own comment.

I hop up on to the counter, picking up a can of lager that I'd stashed between the pens and the PDQ machine and cracking the top. I tap it a few times with a pencil, the chime marking the start of ceremonies, and the customers gather to watch me on my makeshift podium. Karen announces with a slur that she'll happily finish any more beers I have. The crowd laughs. Some of them look unsteady, a little glazed, wolfing down my wine as they are. These people will drink anything, literally anything.

'Theydies and gentlethems,' I say in my mandated gender-neutral corporate speak, 'I want to thank you all on behalf of Companionz Petz for coming along

the great deals he'd sorted. I'd just nodded and congratulated him that he was doing a fine job.

I'd overheard him on a call when he'd thought I'd been out of earshot. He was having a good joke about things. 'Nah, it's okay,' he'd laughed down the phone, 'I won't take you outside and shoot you if it's no good.'

We advertised the event on social media. Drinks at Companionz Petz, one evening promo and discount offers, join our rebrand, be a part of our rebrand, over-18s only, limited spaces, first come/first served. It was the most shared post I'd ever stuck up. Even some asshole in North America was plugging it.

***

I decide that there are enough of us in the store.

Tony necks his drink in a long gulp and heads off toward the fish section. Karen lingers a moment longer, upending the last dregs of wine into her mouth before lifting yet another plastic cup, then waddles off behind him. I pull the doors closed, tinkering with the switch above the sliding opening, locking the two glass jaws together so that nobody else can join our soiree. Eighty of us is plenty, and I slip a sign on the glass in Sellotape. Event full. Sorry.

Many of the customers already look tipsy as I walk through to the service desk at the back of the store, tonight. I know it's going to be special...'

'It's going to be cheap!' a stray voice cuts me off, and a fresh round of laughter rumbles at head level, three feet below where I am standing.

'But seriously,' I say after a pause, 'as you know we had an incident a while back with one of our staff, a good friend of mine, Chris Grindle...'

Jobe locks on to me from mid-crowd, unable to believe his luck. He will be on the phone at the first chance, dobbing me to head office for this, an unexpected opportunity to bolster his claim for the manager's role. Toward the back of the punters, I see a woman with a confused expression glance at her husband. He looks at her, pops two fingers into his mouth, jerks his head back. She sees that I see this and she taps him on the elbow, bringing him back in line.

'I just ask that we can, in fond memory of Chris, just take a drink. To Chris.'

There's a low but disjointed chorus from the customers. Some of them say it, some of them say 'To Chris,' but most don't. They look awkward as they sip their drinks, wanting to be anywhere but under my gaze as I police them into the toast.

I let the silence linger a moment, revel in it until I invite Jobe to take the stage. He cuts me a toxic glance in passing, and I trade him a shit-eating grin in return, but he performs like the perfect retail puppet on the counter, reeling off the cheap-cheap offers to come tonight. His audience trills. I fetch more wine from the store room, hungry eyes following the already opened bottles in my hand, and I pass them around, letting the customers help themselves. 'Drink up,' I say, 'drink up.'

Jobe is still speaking as I head over to the fish section to watch the guppies with their billowing tails. A lone female has jumped from her own single-sex aquarium into a tank full of males, and they are chasing her, waving their sexual organs, frenzied and single-minded and they look so stupid, so utterly, God damned stupid doing that, but it's enough to make a man chuckle. ∎

Contributors

Ivan Mikolji is a world-renowned river explorer and audio-visual artist. The philosophy that moves his creative will is the urgency to preserve the aquatic ecosystems of the planet, and as a first step he considers it necessary to make the richness and beauty of these biomes known to all. Find more of his work at *www.mikolji.com*

Frank Magallanes' interest in piranhas began as a youngster in 1957 when he saw them in a comic book called The Phantom. From that day forward, he has devoted all of his free time to their research.

Jason Rainbow has been importing fish to the U.K. for the last 26 years and is now privileged to work for the largest freshwater wholesaler in England.

Tim Smith's history with fishes can traced from his first goldfish to his ichthyological academic years, through to his current job as a public aquarist. Growing up on the warm and diverse South African east coast, almost every aspect of his professional and private life has been submerged in the aquatic world. He wouldn't have it any other way.

Sayantani Mahapatra is an Indian food blogger. For the last fourteen years she has been curating old forgotten Bengali recipes on her blog A Homemaker's Diary. She enjoys spreading knowledge about her culture and food with interesting historical and mythological anecdotes. Try more of her recipes at *www.ahomemakersdiary.com*

Teuthis is a secretive artist with a background in oceanography who lives below the radar somewhere on the coastline of France. You can find more of his fabulous pictures at *www.instagram.com/_teuthis_*

Neale Monks studied zoology at Aberdeen, and after a short stint as a marine biologist mostly counting polychaete worms from the mud around oil rigs, he moved into palaeontology at the Natural History Museum in London.

Max Pedley is the director of Ornamental Aquatics Wholesale and a regular contributor to aquarium publications. As well as being a highly regarded hobbyist and fish breeder, he has spent time working in both aquatic retail and the education sector.

Kenton Geer is a sea captain, author, and the owner of Vicious Cycle Fisheries in Hawaii. His book 'Vicious Cycle: Whiskey, Women and Water' is currently available at *www.whiskeywomenwater.com*, while more of his writing and photos can be found over on *www.instagram.com/viciouscyclefishing*

Bryce Risley is a US based marine social ecologist and photographer who specialises in science communication and research. Risley's work in the aquarium trade has informed his critiques of industry and how science is applied in policy. He has delivered lectures on fishery and aquaculture related topics at public aquariums, universities, and international conferences.

Steven Grant is a UK aquarist and amateur ichthyologist who specialises in catfish. He has authored a book and numerous articles for aquarium publications. He is the Editor of the Journal of the Catfish Study Group, and an international speaker at conventions. Steve has described numerous taxa and has a *Corydoras* catfish species named after him.

Nathan Hill is a magazine editor, writer and fishkeeper. He misses his dog, Goose, to whom he dedicates this magazine.

Graeme Rigby has done poetry gigs, jazz opera, radio, documentary and fiction. He'll still do any of that as long as it's about herring. In 2020, he launched Rigby's Encyclopaedia of the Herring at *www.herripedia.com*

Joshua Pickett is a visual science communicator with a love of 'unloveable' wildlife. It's his belief that by celebrating wildlife through art and literature, we elevate it to somewhere we sympathise with easier. For this reason, he's publishing a series of books, starting with the increasingly vulnerable and ancient bichir fish, available at *www.thebichirhandbook.com*

Dorian Noel illustrated The Bichir Handbook. He studied biology, ecology and ichthyology. He is fascinated by the creation and construction processes of an illustration, using watercolour, gouache, pencil, and ink to represent unique scenes or rare organisms. See more of his illustrations at *www.artstation.com/donooo*

Ian Hodgson is an award-winning editor and author. After training at the Royal Botanical Gardens Kew, he worked as Editor of The Garden magazine, and Editor in Chief for the Royal Horticultural Society. He is now Editor at Large for the magazines Garden News and Garden Answers.

Madhusudhan Gundappa is a mechanical engineer based in Italy. He is a part time illustrator specialised in generating detailed illustrations of fish species. You can check out his artwork on twitter (@fish_lines). Beyond this, he is also a big fan of aquariums and fishkeeping.